THE ASIA–PACIFIC ROAD SAFETY OBSERVATORY'S INDICATORS FOR MEMBER COUNTRIES

JUNE 2022

ASIAN DEVELOPMENT BANK

ADB

© 2022 Asian Development Bank
6 ADB Avenue, Mandaluyong City, 1550 Metro Manila, Philippines
Tel +63 2 8632 4444; Fax +63 2 8636 2444
www.adb.org

Some rights reserved. Published in 2022.

ISBN 978-92-9269-355-8 (print); 978-92-9269-356-5 (electronic); 978-92-9269-357-2 (ebook)
Publication Stock No. SPR220031
DOI: http://dx.doi.org/10.22617/SPR220031

The views expressed in this publication are those of the authors and do not necessarily reflect the views and policies of the Asian Development Bank (ADB) or its Board of Governors or the governments they represent.

ADB does not guarantee the accuracy of the data included in this publication and accepts no responsibility for any consequence of their use. The mention of specific companies or products of manufacturers does not imply that they are endorsed or recommended by ADB in preference to others of a similar nature that are not mentioned.

By making any designation of or reference to a particular territory or geographic area, or by using the term "country" in this document, ADB does not intend to make any judgments as to the legal or other status of any territory or area.

Please contact pubsmarketing@adb.org if you have questions or comments with respect to content, or if you wish to obtain copyright permission for your intended use that does not fall within these terms, or for permission to use the ADB logo.

Corrigenda to ADB publications may be found at http://www.adb.org/publications/corrigenda.

Notes:
In this publication, "$" refers to United States dollars.
ADB recognizes "Vietnam" as Viet Nam.

On the cover: Various road safety conditions and interventions—such as the presence of crossing guards, placement of safety signs, and maintenance works—across Asia and the Pacific (photos by ADB).

Contents

Tables and Figures

Acknowledgments

This report was prepared by Charles Melhuish, road safety specialist, and Mirick Paala, road crash database specialist. Production of this report by the Asian Development Bank (ADB) is intended to support the work of the Asia–Pacific Road Safety Observatory Secretariat located at the ADB headquarters in Manila, Philippines, with funding from ADB and UK Aid through the Global Road Safety Facility.

Thoughtful comments were received from James Leather and Michael Anyala of ADB, Maria Segui-Gomez of the Federation Internationale de l'Automobile Foundation, Alina Burlacu and Veronica Raffo of the World Bank, Greg Smith of the International Road Assessment Program, Veronique Feypell of the International Transport Forum, and Blaise Murphet of the Global Road Safety Partnership.

Abbreviations

ADB	Asian Development Bank
APRSO	Asia-Pacific Road Safety Observatory
BAC	blood alcohol concentration
CADaS	Common Accident Data Set
CARE	Common Accident Road Database
EU	European Union
GRSP	Global Road Safety Partnership
iRAP	International Road Assessment Programme
IRTAD	International Traffic Safety Data and Analysis Group of the International Transport Forum
MMUCC	Model Minimum Uniform Crash Criteria
NCAP	New Car Assessment Program
PIARC	World Road Association (Permanent International Association of Road Congresses)
SPI	safety performance indicator
UN	United Nations
WHO	World Health Organization

1. Introduction

The Asia–Pacific Road Safety Observatory (APRSO) is the regional forum on road safety data, policies, and practices to ensure the protection of human life on roads across Asia and the Pacific. Its mission is to support countries to generate robust road safety data and analysis to positively impact on policies and actions for road safety in the region.

APRSO provides a platform for decision-makers from countries in the region to share experiences and learn about best practices to address the ongoing road safety epidemic. One of the major outputs of the observatory is a report prepared by a task force on a minimum set of indicators for road safety.[1] This report utilized the work of the task force in its preparation.

The key objectives of this report are to assess and recommend data to be collected and used at the national level as well as asses the data to be shared with the APRSO by member countries.

Chapter 2 establishes the conceptual framework in developing and organizing the indicators. Chapter 3 proposes crash data elements to be collected at the national level. Chapter 4 recommends crash data reporting to the APRSO. Chapter 5 discusses safety performance indicators (SPIs) at the national level, and Chapter 6 details SPIs at the regional level. Finally, Chapter 7 discusses process and implementation indicators for both the national and regional levels.

---

[1] Asia-Pacific Road Safety Observatory. 2020. *Minimum Set of Indicators*. https://www.unescap.org/sites/default/files/Crash-related%20 minimum%20data%20set%20and%20data%20sources.pdf.

2. Conceptual Framework

What Are Indicators?

Indicators and combinations of indicators, in general, are used to reveal, measure, and understand a particular issue or area of interest.[2] The types of indicators, and how to collect and analyze them are heavily dependent on context and objective (footnote 2). The Sustainable Urban Mobility Plan (SUMP) handbook defines the characteristics of indicators to include being well-defined, having existing knowledge available, being easily understandable, having clear definitions for each indicator, identifying a baseline value, setting target values, and taking into account data sources.[3] In addition, an indicator is a metric for progress (or the lack of it), and it is crucial and instrumental to the development of necessary interventions and programs (footnote 3).

The selection of indicators for a particular field is not a simple task. For one, there is no single variable that can account for and cover complex issues such as road safety. On the other hand, numerous and complicated indicators can cause information overload which can hamper efficiency and efficacy in decision-making.[4] Therefore, having a few indicators that can be reliably and accurately collected and that can sufficiently account for a field of interest is ideal.

There is also an issue of data quality and availability. Indicators must be identified and customized based on the capacity and resources of data collectors and assessors. Every institution operates differently—at a different scale and level, with a different set of actors, with different mandates—and these should be considered when developing indicators (footnote 2). Conducting intensive stakeholder consultations and workshops are helpful to address this issue.[5]

Finally, indicators must be relevant and appropriate, and must provide compelling information that warrants the need for collecting them (footnote 3).

There are many ways to categorize indicators (footnote 2). They can be based on the following:
* Dimension in which the indicator moves (i.e. time, space)
* Complexity of the messages conveyed by the indicator
    > Descriptive: give a clear illustration of a condition using a particular variable
    > Efficiency: divide at least two variables with one another to derive a ratio

---

[2] H. Gudmundsson et al. 2016. *Sustainable Transportation: Indicators, Frameworks, and Performance Management.* Berlin Heidelberg: Springer-Verlag.

[3] A. Gühnemann. 2016. *SUMP Manual on Monitoring and Evaluation: Assessing the Impact of Measures and Evaluating Mobility Planning Processes.* www.sump-challenges.eu/kits.

[4] R. Congelton and W. Sweetser. 1992. Political Deadlocks and Distributional Information: The Value of the Veil. *Public Choice,* 73, 1–19.

[5] D. Hills and K. Junge. 2010. *Guidance for Transport Impact Evaluations: Choosing an Evaluation Approach to Achieve Better Attribution.* UK: Tavistock Institute.

- > Normative: help assess a problem using a standard, threshold, criterion, or target
- > Index or total welfare: combine multiple indicators
- Positions of the indicator before or after the events it indicates
  - > Leading: predict the peaks and troughs
  - > Lagging: occur after the fact
- Stages in a process that the indicator can support—combination of previous indicators including overall level, scale, and time frame of their applicability in the process of producing or maintaining a certain service or product
  - > Input
  - > Output
  - > Outcome
  - > Efficiency (Input/Output)
  - > Effectiveness (Targets/Outcomes)

The choice of the type of indicator is mainly based on the framework from which it exists. In this case, road safety indicators and crash data elements will be collected at the national and regional levels for the APRSO.

Framework for Identifying Road Safety Indicators

Frameworks are tools to identify and organize indicators (footnote 2). There are three documents that can inform the choice of indicators for the APRSO. One is the *Voluntary Global Targets for Road Safety*, which was finalized by the World Health Organization (WHO) in November 2017. These global targets have been developed by WHO in consultation and coordination with its member states and key stakeholders, the results of which are 12 targets that aim to reduce road crash fatalities and injuries.[6] These global targets are enumerated in Table 1.

The other crucial document is the United Nations (UN) Resolution 74/299 adopted by the General Assembly on 31 August 2020 and echoed by the current draft of the Global Action Plan for Road Safety 2021–2030. The UN resolution, as well as the Global Action Plan for Road Safety 2021–2030, sets a 50% target reduction of road crash fatalities and injuries by 2030. The document also reaffirms the need for activities to be guided by the safe systems approach and Vision Zero.[7]

The Global Road Safety Facility has developed guidelines in road safety management.[8] These guidelines provide a framework which identifies the different aspects of road safety and how they relate with each other. Three elements are identified: institutional management functions, interventions, and results.

Institutional management functions comprise coordination, legislation, funding and resource allocation, promotion, monitoring and evaluation, research and development, and knowledge transfer. These institutional functions act as the base of an effective road safety management strategy and when fulfilled, will translate to interventions.

Interventions refer to the safety measures applied to the road and its environment, as well as to the vehicle, road user, and the recovery and rehabilitation of crash victims. Interventions are focused on the road networks where crashes occur. Effective interventions will produce appropriate safety outcomes.

---

[6] WHO. 2017. *Global Road Safety Performance Targets*. https://www.who.int/violence_injury_prevention/road_traffic/12GlobalRoadSafetyTargets.pdf
[7] UN General Assembly. 2020. *UN Resolution 74/299*. https://undocs.org/en/A/RES/74/299.
[8] T. Bliss and J. Breen . 2013. *Implementing the Recommendations of the World Report: Road Safety Management Capacity Reviews and Safe System Projects Guidelines* (English). Washington DC: World Bank Group.

Table 1   Voluntary Global Targets for Road Safety

Number	Target
1	By 2020, all countries should establish a comprehensive multisector national road safety action plan with time-bound targets.
2	By 2030, all countries should accede to one or more of the core road safety-related United Nations legal instruments.
3	By 2030, all new roads should achieve technical standards for all road users that take into account road safety, or meet a three-star rating or better.
4	By 2030, more than 75% of travel on existing roads is on roads that meet the technical standards that take into account road safety for all road users.
5	By 2030, 100% of new (defined as produced, sold, or imported) and used vehicles should meet high-quality safety standards, such as the recommended priority United Nations regulations, Global Technical Regulations, or the equivalent recognized national performance requirements.
6	By 2030, halve the proportion of vehicles traveling over the posted speed limit and achieve a reduction in speed-related injuries and fatalities.
7	By 2030, increase the proportion of motorcycle riders correctly using standard helmets to close to 100%
8	By 2030, increase the proportion of motor vehicle occupants using safety belts or child restraint systems to close to 100%.
9	By 2030, halve the number of road traffic injuries and fatalities related to drivers using alcohol and/or achieve a reduction in those related to other psychoactive substances.
10	By 2030, all countries should have national laws to restrict or prohibit the use of mobile phones while driving.
11	By 2030, all countries should enact regulation for driving time and rest periods for professional drivers, and/or accede to international/regional regulation in this area.
12	By 2030, all countries should establish and achieve national targets in order to minimize the time interval between road traffic crash and the provision of first professional emergency care.

Source: Asia-Pacific Road Safety Observatory, 2021.

It has to be emphasized that results do not only refer to the number of fatalities and injuries which are identified as the final outcomes. There are also intermediate outcomes (performance indicators) such as traffic speeds and outputs such as the number of safe infrastructure. At every level of the road safety management framework, a set of indicators can be developed.

The three documents provide a basis for the development of regional indicators for the APRSO as well as national indicators for the member countries. National and regional indicators can be developed in alignment with the global targets provided by the United Nations in the *Voluntary Global Targets for Road Safety* and the target 50% reduction in fatalities and injuries in the UN Resolution 74/299, as well as the draft Global Action Plan for Road Safety 2021–2030. These indicators can be organized through the Road Safety Management Framework, particularly the outcome indicators or crash data, safety performance indicators, and implementation indicators found on the topmost part of the pyramid in Figure 1. Figure 2 summarizes this conceptual framework and provides an overall picture on how the report is structured.

Figure 1   Road Safety Management Framework

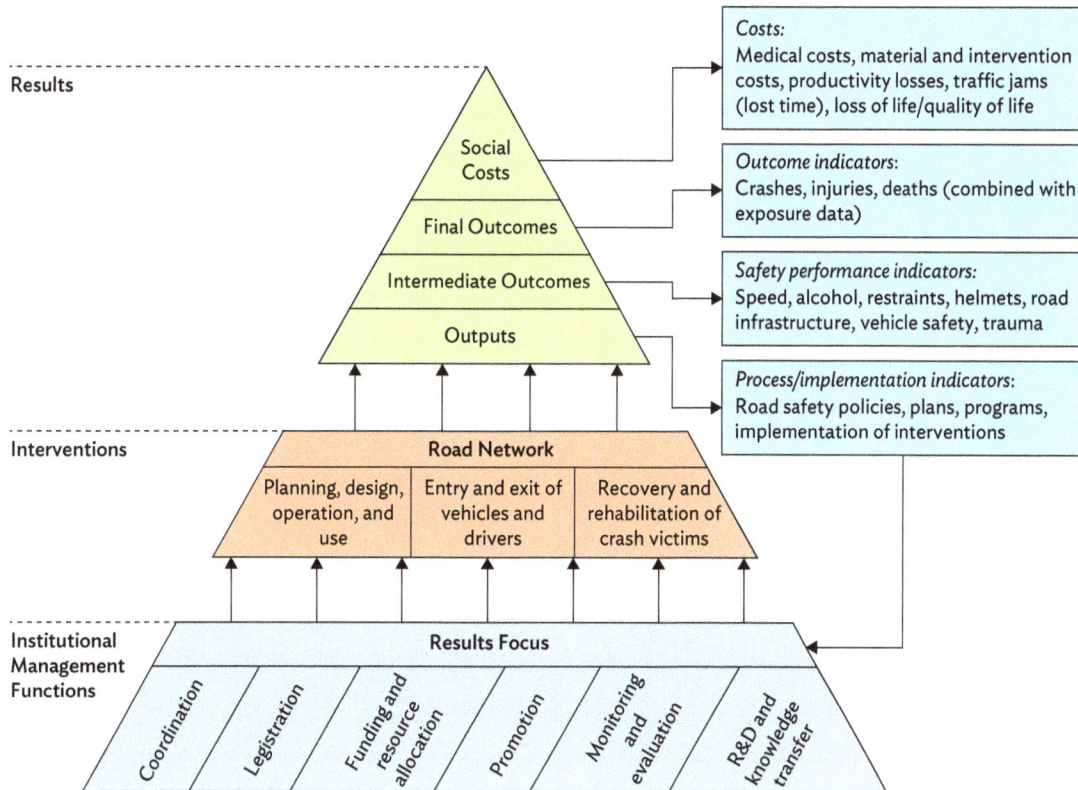

R&D = research and development.
Source: World Bank, 2013.

Figure 2   Conceptual Framework for Developing Road Safety Indicators

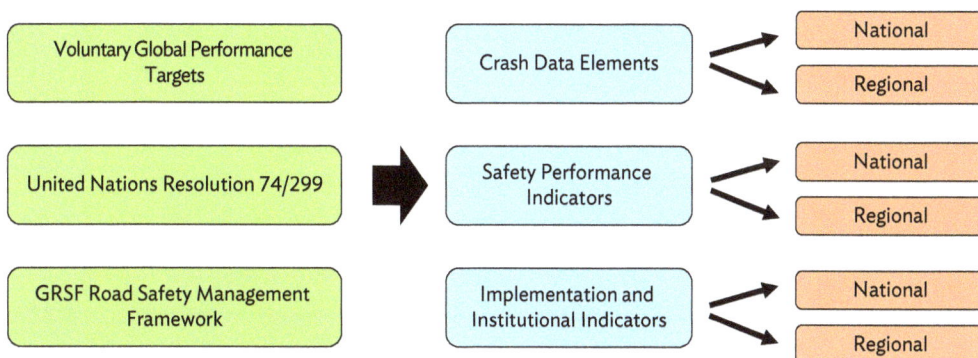

APRSO = Asia–Pacific Road Safety Observatory, GRSF = Global Road Safety Facility.
Source: APRSO, 2021.

3. Crash Data Elements at the National Level

Issues in Crash Reporting

While the target to reduce fatalities and injuries by 50% by 2030 has been defined, it is difficult to monitor progress because of the severe underreporting of road crashes. According to WHO, there is still no robust data on road traffic fatalities and injuries.[9] This is a result of the lack of robust vital registration systems in countries as well as the lack of quality police data. Official fatality data from countries often have large discrepancies from fatality estimates of WHO (Figure 3).

Figure 3   **Comparison of Reported Road Deaths and WHO Estimates across Regions, 2018**

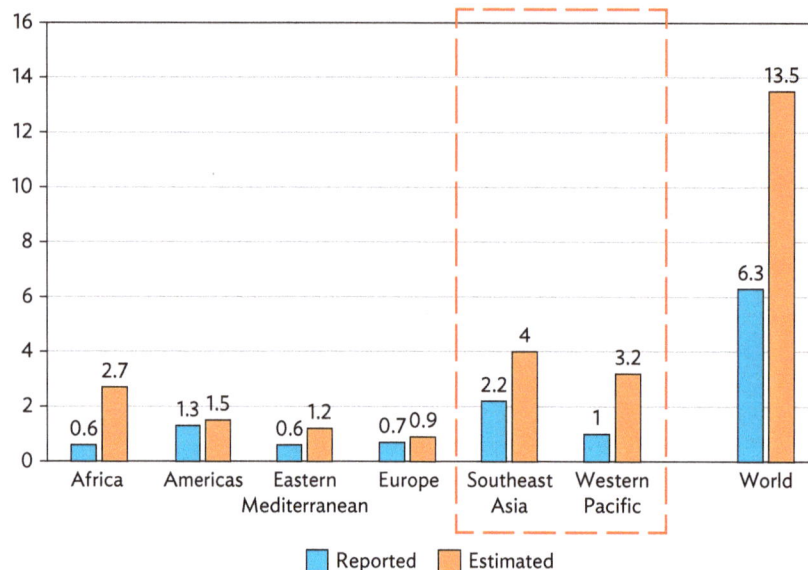

WHO = World Health Organization.
Source: WHO. 2018.

Another issue is the poor coordination between authorities and lack of integration of police and health data in most countries. In a study made by WHO, health and police data have significantly different figures for fatalities and injuries (footnote 9).

---

9   WHO. 2018. *Global Status Report on Road Safety 2018*. Geneva: World Health Organization.

Table 2   Utilization of Crash Data Elements in Crash Reporting in the Philippines, 2020

Data Field	Number of Responses	Response Rate
Driver error	246	18.85%
License number	589	45.13%
Last name	1,283	98.31%
First name	1,289	98.77%
Middle name	1,127	86.36%
Gender	1,271	97.31%
Age	1,137	87.13%
Address	1,238	94.87%
Involvement	1,295	99.23%
Injury	755	57.85%
Hospital	459	35.17%
Alcohol/drugs suspected	90	6.90%
Seatbelt/helmet worn	145	11.11%

Source: University of the Philippines Diliman, 2020.

This is also supported by individual country-level research and studies. Health and police data have been shown to vary widely especially in terms of defining fatalities. Hospitals usually follow the international guidance on defining fatalities as happening within 30 days of a crash, while police often define fatalities as occurring between 24 hours and 7 days.[10] This is a common issue in crash data reporting in several countries in Asia and the Pacific and is a significant issue in preparing comparisons between countries. The differences in definition also apply to other data fields such as the proper identification of injury severity. While the Maximum Abbreviated Injury Score (MAIS) has the most appropriate and objective set of injury severity (six levels), its use is still limited. Other definitions for injury severity include days spent in the hospital and the subjective assessment done by the police.

Several experts have also pointed out that police data are often unreliable especially concerning contributory factors in crashes,[11] and one of the reasons is the lack of well-defined crash data elements designed for certain road user groups such as cyclists.[12] In a recent study in the Philippines,[13] some crash data elements are often left blank when recording crashes. Table 2 shows an example of crash data elements and the percentage of utilization in data forms.

Other outstanding observations in data collection across Asia and the Pacific include the following:
- Police and hospitals often use manual forms which are open to interpretation and errors. Some fields have no assigned values, so data are not standardized. Handwriting can also be illegible, and the form itself vulnerable to loss or damage. All these can lead to incorrect data being uploaded into the system.
- Locations are not exactly identified, usually due to a lack of devices to accurately record location. Location data are often recorded as road or street names, which do not not help the identification of high-risk locations.
- The whole data collection process is tedious and complicated for the police. Forms often include over 80 indicators and can be as long as four pages, which police often have trouble completing because of their lack of capacity, training, and resources.
- There is an overall lack of data quality assurance measures. Once the police record a crash, this is often not updated anymore and will not be cross-checked with other datasets such as hospital records.

---

[10] N. Duc et al. 2011. Study on Quality of Existing Traffic Accident Data in Vietnam. *Proceedings of the Eastern Asia Society for Transportation Studies, 8.* https://www.academia.edu/4140898/Study_on_Quality_of_Existing_Traffic_Accident_Data_in_Vietnam.

[11] A. Montella et al. 2012. Critical Review of the International Crash Databases and Proposals for Improvement of the Italian National Database. *Procedia - Social and Behavioral Sciences, 53*, pp. 49–61. https://www.sciencedirect.com/science/article/pii/S1877042812043212.

[12] J. Rolison. 2020. Identifying the Causes of Road Traffic Collisions: Using Police Officers' Expertise to Improve the Reporting of Contributory Factors Data. *Accident Analysis and Prevention.* https://www.sciencedirect.com/science/article/pii/S0001457519311650.

[13] A. Valdez. 2020. *Evaluation of Electronic Road Incident Record Application and Trial in the Philippines.* Manila: Intelligent Transport System Laboratory, University of the Philippines Diliman.

- The main cause of crashes is mostly recorded as human error. Because crash data reporting is done primarily for prosecution purposes and not really for assessing road safety, there is a requirement to identify 'victims' and 'suspects' and ascribe fault to one of the parties involved in a crash.
- Other datasets are not leveraged. Crash data are not integrated with road infrastructure data, health data, and licensing and vehicle registration data.

Crash Data Elements Collected at the National Level in the Literature

WHO published *Data Systems: A Road Safety Manual for Decision-Makers and Practitioners*[14] in September 2010. This publication was prepared by the Federation Internationale de l'Automobile (FIA) Foundation, the Global Road Safety Partnership (GRSP), WHO, and the World Bank. It consists of four chapters all focusing on road safety data: (1) why are road safety data needed; (2) how to construct a situational assessment; (3) how to design, improve, and implement data systems; and (4) using data to improve road safety. The manual provides detailed advice on how to design, improve, and implement data systems involving key stakeholders in a country. A common dataset and minimum data elements are enumerated in the manual. An overview of minimum crash data elements is shown in Figure 4.

Figure 4   **Minimum Crash Data Elements**

Crash-Related	Road-Related	Vehicle-Related	Person-Related
• Crash identifier (unique reference number assigned to the crash, usually by police) • Crash data • Crash time • Crash municipality/place • Crash location • Crash type • Impact type • Weather conditions • Light conditions • Crash severity°	• Type of roadway* • Road functional class* • Speed limit* • Road obstacles • Road surface conditions* • Junction • Traffic control at junction* • Road curve* • Road segment grade*	• Vehicle number • Vehicle type† • Vehicle make† • Vehicle model† • Vehicle model year† • Engine size† • Vehicle special function† • Vehicle maneuver (what the vehicle was doing at the time of the crash)	• Person ID • Occupant's vehicle number • Pedestrian's linked vehicle number • Date of birth • Sex • Type of road user • Seating position • Injury severity • Safety equipment • Pedestrian manuever • Alcohol use suspected • Alcohol test • Drug use • Driving license issue date • Age°

° Derived or calculated from other data elements.

* Depending on the quality and detail of road inventory and hardware data available, it may be possible to obtain this data element through linkage to other databases.

† Depending on the existence, quality, and detail of a motor vehicle registration database, it may be possible to obtain this data element through linkage to motor vehicle registration files.

Source: World Health Organization, 2010.

---

14   WHO. 2010. *Data Systems: A Road Safety Manual for Decision-Makers and Practitioners.* https://www.who.int/roadsafety/projects/manuals/data/en/.

WHO recommends generating 15 of the 42 data elements in its guide from existing sources such as the vehicle registration database and road infrastructure database. This would result in at least 27 data fields to be collected at the crash scene.

An additional set of elements is also recommended by WHO (Figure 5).

Figure 5   Additional Crash Data Elements

Crash-Related	Road-Related	Vehicle-Related	Person-Related
• Location relative to roadway	• Urban area • Tunnel • Bridge • Number of lanes • Markings • Work-zone related	• Vehicle identification number (VIN, issued by manufacturer) • Registration place and year • Registration number • First point of impact • Insurance • Hazardous materials	• Distracted by device • Driver license class and jurisdiction • Driver manuever • Trip/journey purpose

Source: World Health Organization, 2010.

This additional set, while optional, can be helpful in understanding crashes. In addition to a list of data elements, WHO also provides more details on each of the data fields.

National Highway Traffic Safety Administration, United States—Model Minimum Uniform Crash Criteria

In 2017, an updated version of the Model Minimum Uniform Crash Criteria (MMUCC)[15] was published. The MMUCC is a guideline set by the United States (US) Department of Transportation to standardize crash reporting in the different states. This list is a result of a collaboration between the National Highway Traffic Safety Administration; Federal Highway Administration; Federal Motor Carrier Safety Administration; National Transportation Safety Board; Governors Highway Safety Association; and experts from state departments of transportation, local law enforcement, emergency medical services, safety organizations, industry partners, and academia. There were also online public consultations that were organized to finalize the list.

The MMUCC list of data elements comprises 115 data fields with the following categories: crash details, vehicle details, person details, and road details. Particular types of crashes also have additional data reporting fields such as for fatal crashes, large vehicles and hazardous materials, non-motorists, and dynamic data (footnote 15). Page 1 of the 12-page sample crash data form is provided in Figure 6.

It has to be noted that the data elements in the MMUCC is customized for the US context and policies and might not be relevant for other countries.

[15]   US Department of Transportation and National Highway Traffic Safety Administration. 2017. *Model Minimum Uniform Crash Criteria Fifth Edition* (2017). https://www.nhtsa.gov/mmucc-1.

Figure 6   Page 1 of MMUCC Crash Report

MMUCC CRASH REPORT

CRASH DATA ELEMENTS

C1. Crash Identifier

C2. Crash Classification

S1 Ownership
01 Public Property
02 Private Property

S2 Characteristics
01 Trafficway, On Road
02 Trafficway, Not on Road
03 Non-Trafficway

S3 Secondary Crash?
01 No
02 Yes

C3. Crash Date and Time

S1 Crash Date and Time *(YYYYMMDDHHMM)*

S2 Time of Roadway Clearance *(HHMM)*

C4. Crash County

C5. Crash City/Place *(Political Jurisdiction)*

C6. Crash Location
Latitude *(degrees.minutes.seconds + compass direction)*
Longitude *(degrees.minutes.seconds + compass direction)*

C7. First Harmful Event

Non-Collision Harmful Events
01 Cargo/Equipment Loss or Shift
02 Fell/Jumped From Motor Vehicle
03 Fire/Explosion
04 Immersion, Full or Partial
05 Jackknife
06 Other Non-Collision
07 Overturn/Rollover
08 Thrown or Falling Object

Collision With Person, Motor Vehicle, or Non-Fixed Object
09 Animal *(live)*
10 Construction Equipment *(backhoe, bulldozer, etc.)*
11 Farm Equipment *(tractor, combine harvester, etc.)*
12 Motor Vehicle in Transport
13 Other Non-Fixed Object
14 Other Non-motorist
15 Parked Motor Vehicle
16 Pedalcycle
17 Pedestrian
18 Railway Vehicle *(train, engine)*
19 Strikes Object at Rest from MV in Transport
20 Struck by Falling, Shifting Cargo or Anything Set in Motion by Motor Vehicle

Collision With Fixed Object
21 Bridge Overhead Structure
22 Bridge Pier or Support
23 Bridge Rail
24 Cable Barrier
25 Concrete Traffic Barrier
26 Culvert
27 Curb
28 Ditch
29 Embankment
30 Fence
31 Guardrail End Terminal
32 Guardrail Face
33 Impact Attenuator/Crash Cushion
34 Mailbox
35 Other Fixed Object *(wall, building, tunnel, etc.)*
36 Other Post, Pole, or Support
37 Other Traffic Barrier
38 Traffic Sign Support
39 Traffic Signal Support
40 Tree *(standing)*
41 Utility Pole/Light Support

99 Unknown

C8. Location of First Harmful Event Relative to the Trafficway
01 Gore
02 In Parking Lane or Zone
03 Median
04 Off-Roadway, Location Unknown
05 On Roadway
06 On Shoulder, Left Side
07 On Shoulder, Right Side
08 Outside Road/Right-of-Way
09 Roadside
10 Separator/Traffic Island

99 Unknown

C9. Manner of Crash/Collision Impact
00 Not a Collision Between Two Motor Vehicles

01 Angle
02 Front to Front
03 Front to Rear
04 Rear to Rear
05 Rear to Side
06 Sideswipe, Opposite Direction
07 Sideswipe, Same Direction

98 Other
99 Unknown

C10. Source of Information

S1 Source of Information
01 Law Enforcement Agency
02 Civilian

S2 Law Enforcement Agency Identifier
9 characters   NCIC Originating Agency Identifier (OAI)

999999997   Not Applicable

C11. Weather Conditions *(choose up to 2)*
01 Blowing Sand, Soil, Dirt
02 Blowing Snow
03 Clear
04 Cloudy
05 Fog, Smog, Smoke
06 Freezing Rain or Freezing Drizzle
07 Rain
08 Severe Crosswinds
09 Sleet or Hail
10 Snow

98 Other
99 Unknown

C12. Light Condition
01 Daylight
02 Dawn/Dusk
03 Dark – Lighted
04 Dark – Not Lighted
05 Dark – Unknown Lighting
98 Other
99 Unknown

C13. Roadway Surface Condition
01 Dry
02 Ice/Frost
03 Mud, Dirt, Gravel
04 Oil
05 Sand
06 Slush
07 Snow
08 Water *(standing, moving)*
09 Wet
98 Other
99 Unknown

C14. Contributing Circumstances – Roadway Environment *(choose up to 2)*
00 None
01 Animal(s)
02 Debris
03 Glare
04 Non-Highway Work
05 Obstructed Crosswalks
06 Obstruction in Roadway
07 Prior Crash
08 Prior Non-Recurring Incident
09 Regular Congestion
10 Related to a Bus Stop
11 Road Surface Condition *(wet, icy, snow, slush, etc.)*
12 Ruts, Holes, Bumps
13 Shoulders *(none, low, soft, high)*
14 Toll Booth/Plaza Related
15 Traffic Control Device
16 Traffic Incident
17 Visual Obstruction(s)
18 Weather Conditions
19 Work Zone *(construction/maintenance/utility)*
20 Worn, Travel-polished Surface

98 Other
99 Unknown

C15. Relation to Junction

S1 Within Interchange Area?
01 No
02 Yes

99 Unknown

S2 Specific Location
00 Not an Interchange Area

01 Acceleration/Deceleration Lane
02 Crossover-Related
03 Driveway Access or Related
04 Entrance/Exit Ramp or Related
05 Intersection or Related
06 Non-Junction
07 Railway Grade Crossing
08 Shared-Use Path or Trail
09 Through Roadway

10 Other Location Not Listed Above Within an Interchange Area *(median, shoulder and roadside)*

99 Unknown

C16. Type of Intersection

S1 Number of Approaches
00 Not an Intersection
02 (2) Two
03 (3) Three
04 (4) Four
05 (5+) Five or more

S2 Overall Intersection Geometry
00 Angled/Skewed
02 Roundabout/Traffic Circle
03 Perpendicular

97 Not Applicable/Not an Intersection

S3 Overall Traffic Control Device
01 Signalized
02 Stop – All Way
03 Stop – Partial
04 Yield
05 No Controls

97 Not Applicable/Not an Intersection

C17. School Bus-Related
01 No
02 Yes, School Bus Directly Involved
03 Yes, School Bus Indirectly Involved

🔗 Linked or Derived   **S#** Subfield Number

❶

MMUC = Model Minimum Uniform Crash Criteria.

Source: United States Department of Transportation and National Highway Traffic Safety Administration. 2017.

European Union: Common Accident Data Set

The Common Accident Data Set (CADaS) aims to standardize the definitions and collection of crash data elements throughout the European Union (EU).[16] It informs the indicators found in the European road crash database system called the Common Accident Road Database (CARE). European countries can voluntarily adopt CADaS for their own individual database systems.

Indicators in CADaS were selected based on the following principles:
- Indicators are relevant and useful in road crash analysis at the EU level.
- Indicators are meant for wider policies and programs instead of crash reconstruction and investigation.
- Countries have the flexibility to customize the dataset based on their capacities and needs.
- Indicators must be easily collected, comprehensive, and concise.
- The dataset only focuses on fatal and injury crashes.

Each data element falls under one of four categories: (1) accident, (2) road-related, (3) traffic unit (vehicle and pedestrian), and (4) person details (footnote 16). A list of all data elements and how they relate to each other is shown in Figure 7.

There are 77 data elements which are divided based on importance: 40 indicators are tagged as high importance and the rest are of low improtance (Table 3).

Table 3   Number of High-Importance and Low-Importance Variables in the Common Accident Data Set

| Category | Code | Number of Variables | | | Number of Values | | |
		High (H) importance	Lower (L) importance	Total	Detailed values	Alternative values (A)	Total
Accident	A	7	6	13	91	13	104
Road	R	12	13	25	92	13	105
Traffic Unit	U	8	10	18	181	15	196
Person	P	13	8	21	92	10	102
Total		40	37	77	456	51	507

Source: European Commission. 2018.

During this pilot, the government has witnessed the power of merely recording crashes onto a map and how this can inform evidence-based decisions in road safety (Figure 14).

---

[16]   European Commission. 2018. *Common Accident Data Set.* https://ec.europa.eu/transport/road_safety/system/files/2021-07/cadas_glossary_v_3_7.pdf.

Figure 7   **List of Crash Data Elements Found in the Common Accident Data Set**

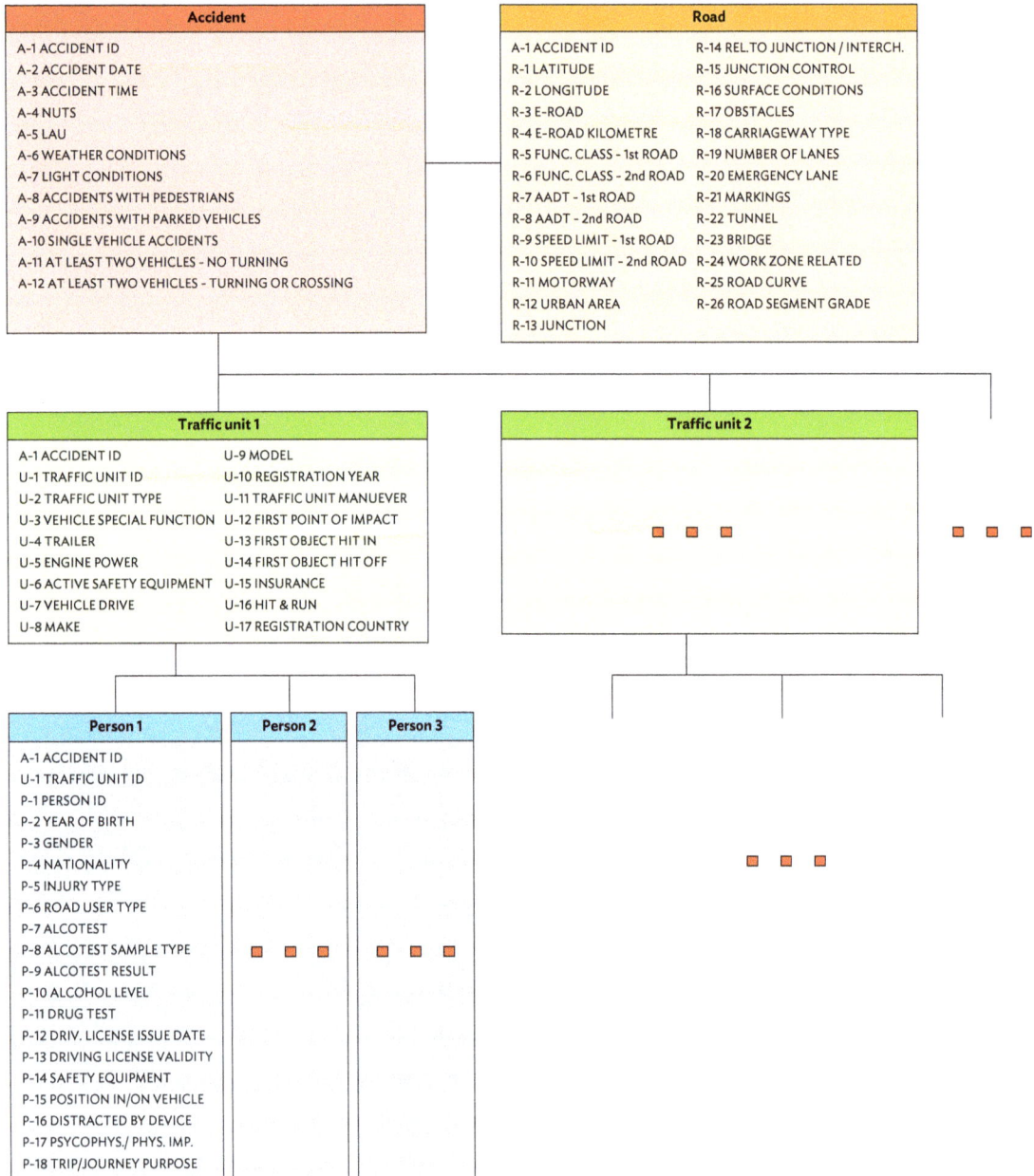

Accident
A-1 ACCIDENT ID
A-2 ACCIDENT DATE
A-3 ACCIDENT TIME
A-4 NUTS
A-5 LAU
A-6 WEATHER CONDITIONS
A-7 LIGHT CONDITIONS
A-8 ACCIDENTS WITH PEDESTRIANS
A-9 ACCIDENTS WITH PARKED VEHICLES
A-10 SINGLE VEHICLE ACCIDENTS
A-11 AT LEAST TWO VEHICLES - NO TURNING
A-12 AT LEAST TWO VEHICLES - TURNING OR CROSSING

Road	
A-1 ACCIDENT ID	R-14 REL.TO JUNCTION / INTERCH.
R-1 LATITUDE	R-15 JUNCTION CONTROL
R-2 LONGITUDE	R-16 SURFACE CONDITIONS
R-3 E-ROAD	R-17 OBSTACLES
R-4 E-ROAD KILOMETRE	R-18 CARRIAGEWAY TYPE
R-5 FUNC. CLASS - 1st ROAD	R-19 NUMBER OF LANES
R-6 FUNC. CLASS - 2nd ROAD	R-20 EMERGENCY LANE
R-7 AADT - 1st ROAD	R-21 MARKINGS
R-8 AADT - 2nd ROAD	R-22 TUNNEL
R-9 SPEED LIMIT - 1st ROAD	R-23 BRIDGE
R-10 SPEED LIMIT - 2nd ROAD	R-24 WORK ZONE RELATED
R-11 MOTORWAY	R-25 ROAD CURVE
R-12 URBAN AREA	R-26 ROAD SEGMENT GRADE
R-13 JUNCTION	

Traffic unit 1	
A-1 ACCIDENT ID	U-9 MODEL
U-1 TRAFFIC UNIT ID	U-10 REGISTRATION YEAR
U-2 TRAFFIC UNIT TYPE	U-11 TRAFFIC UNIT MANUEVER
U-3 VEHICLE SPECIAL FUNCTION	U-12 FIRST POINT OF IMPACT
U-4 TRAILER	U-13 FIRST OBJECT HIT IN
U-5 ENGINE POWER	U-14 FIRST OBJECT HIT OFF
U-6 ACTIVE SAFETY EQUIPMENT	U-15 INSURANCE
U-7 VEHICLE DRIVE	U-16 HIT & RUN
U-8 MAKE	U-17 REGISTRATION COUNTRY

Traffic unit 2

Person 1	Person 2	Person 3
A-1 ACCIDENT ID		
U-1 TRAFFIC UNIT ID		
P-1 PERSON ID		
P-2 YEAR OF BIRTH		
P-3 GENDER		
P-4 NATIONALITY		
P-5 INJURY TYPE		
P-6 ROAD USER TYPE		
P-7 ALCOTEST		
P-8 ALCOTEST SAMPLE TYPE		
P-9 ALCOTEST RESULT		
P-10 ALCOHOL LEVEL		
P-11 DRUG TEST		
P-12 DRIV. LICENSE ISSUE DATE		
P-13 DRIVING LICENSE VALIDITY		
P-14 SAFETY EQUIPMENT		
P-15 POSITION IN/ON VEHICLE		
P-16 DISTRACTED BY DEVICE		
P-17 PSYCOPHYS./ PHYS. IMP.		
P-18 TRIP/JOURNEY PURPOSE		

Source: European Commission. 2018.

African Road Safety Observatory: Recommendations for a Common Data Collection System and Definitions

The recommended minimum set of data elements in Africa was first developed by the EU-funded African Road Safety Observatory. The recommendations were based on WHO's road safety systems guide, the EU's CADaS, and a survey of data collection systems in Africa.[17] A 2018 SaferAfrica report recommends 42 crash data elements which cover accident, road, vehicle, and person-related variables (footnote 17). These indicators are also categorized by first and second priority in terms of data collection. There are 25 first-priority indicators while the rest are second priority. Table 4 shows how the indicators are categorized. A new African Road Safety Observatory was created under the African Union and is also working on establishing a set of indicators for the region.

Table 4   Recommended Variables Organized by First and Second Priority

Accident-Related Variables		Road-Related Variables		Vehicle-Related Variables		Person-Related Variables	
First priority	Second priority	First priority	Second priority	First priority	Second priority	First priority	Second priority
Accident ID	Impact type	Type of roadway	Speed limit	Vehicle number	Engine size	Date of birth	Person ID
Accident date		Road functional class	Road obstacles	Vehicle type	Vehicle special function	Gender	Occupant's vehicle number
Accident time		Junction	Road surface conditions	Vehicle make		Type of road user	Pedestrian's linked vehicle number
Accident region-municipality			Traffic control at junction	Vehicle model		Seating position	Safety equipment
Accident location			Road curve	Vehicle model year		Injury severity	Pedestrian manuever
Accident type			Road segment grade	Vehicle manuever		Driving licence issue date	Alcohol use suspected
Weather conditions						Age	Alcohol test
Light conditions							Drug use
Accident severity							

Source: Thomas, P. et al. 2018. *Recommendations for a Common Data Collection System and Definitions*. SaferAfrica Project. https://www.ssatp.org/sites/ssatp/files/publication/common_data_collection_system_definitions.pdf.

Asia-Pacific Road Safety Observatory: Task Force Document on Minimum Crash Data Elements

The APRSO Task Force on Minimum Crash Data Elements, which is composed of voluntary member countries and international partner organizations, has developed a document identifying minimum crash data elements.[18] The document consists of 49 individual crash data elements with at least 45 indicators tagged as mandatory data elements. The APRSO document is almost similar to the EU-funded set of crash data elements for the African

---

[17] P. Thomas et al. 2018. *Recommendations for a Common Data Collection System and Definitions*. SaferAfrica Project. https://www.ssatp.org/sites/ssatp/files/publication/common_data_collection_system_definitions.pdf.
[18] APRSO. *Minimum Set of Indicators*. https://www.unescap.org/sites/default/files/Crash-related%20minimum%20data%20set%20and%20data%20sources.pdf.

Road Safety Observatory; however, the data elements for the APRSO are unclear regarding mandatory elements as they do not include any tagging. Like previous literature, the document categorizes crashes into crash, road, vehicle, and person-related variables.

Summary of Findings

A literature review of crash data elements yielded these key findings:
- To meet the 50% reduction in fatalities and injuries, there is a strong need to improve the reporting of crash data in Asia and the Pacific to monitor progress and evaluate the impact of different interventions. Institutional arrangements within and between agencies are important to support data collection and management. These include standardization of forms and definitions; sustainable funding; and other related functions such as regular training in data entry, crash investigation, and injury assessment.
- Updating of crash data systems should also consider the use of digital forms and devices as this improves data collection, quality, and ease of subsequent analysis.
- With the exception of the MMUCC, minimum indicators are often categorized by crash-, road-, and vehicle- and person-related variables.
- These categories are further subdivided into high importance or first priority and low importance or second priority, indicating that within a minimum set of indicators, there is still a core or mandatory set of indicators.
- All of the above examples emphasize the flexibility of the dataset and how individual countries must customize and contextualize the indicators based on their capacities and needs. What works in one place cannot simply be copied or applied to another country.
- All have identified the need for collaboration among government ministries and the integration of different datasets and database systems. As much as possible, countries must leverage existing datasets and integrate these with the crash database system such as the road infrastructure database and the licensing and vehicle registration database systems.
- Data collection for road safety monitoring and evaluation should primarily include fatal and injury crashes, and not just property damage crashes.
- Out of all the data elements reviewed, 16 are commonly marked "high importance" or "first priority" among the lists:
  - crash identifier (unique reference)
  - crash date
  - crash time
  - crash location
  - weather conditions
  - light conditions
  - crash severity (in CADaS, it falls under the injury severity category; the MMUCC has different assigned values)
  - road functional class
  - junction type (in the MMUCC, it is in a subfield of junction)
  - vehicle type (in CADaS, it falls under traffic unit type which includes both vehicles and pedestrians)
  - vehicle maneuver (in CADaS, it falls under traffic unit maneuver which includes both vehicle and pedestrian maneuver)
  - date of birth
  - sex/gender
  - type of road user
  - seating position
  - injury severity

Recommended Crash Data Elements Collected at the National Level

The primary goal of collecting data is not to have a perfect dataset but rather a sufficient one that can be collected reliably and accurately, and can be used to inform meaningful decisions on road safety. While there is a large set of crash data elements, not all are equally important and not all are urgently needed to create meaningful interventions. The dataset must strike a balance between information overload and absence of data. In this regard, the proposed minimum crash data elements are selected as part of a program to strengthen data collection and management for the crash database. A gradual approach is proposed for data improvement. As observed in the literature, each member country of the APRSO will need to consider the priority data elements that are appropriate for their jurisdiction. These will help them initiate or improve evidence-based road safety programs even without a complete dataset. It is recommended that the data improvement program be divided into three stages:
1. collecting core crash data elements,
2. expanding the coverage of data collection, and
3. integrating data.

While there are three stages, it does not mean that governments will only collect data elements in one stage before moving on to the next. The stages only signify that data improvement strategies be prioritized for the core data elements before including items on the expanded list and incorporating elements that will require the integration of crash data with other related datasets.

The goal of the first stage is to provide the basic core mandatory elements crucial to a good understanding of safety. This will facilitate the preparation of appropriate remedial actions and countermeasures, as well as implement appropriate road infrastructure treatments. Countries should be able to undertake regular assessments of their performance in collecting these mandatory indicators. Crucial in this stage is the establishment of institutional mechanisms for collecting, analyzing, and sharing data; identifying the necessary complementary equipment such as global positioning system (GPS) devices for the procurement, preparation, and development of a national crash database system; and standardizing the definitions of fatality and injury, among many other tasks. If these parameters are established, then the resulting data and information collected should achieve a reasonable level of accuracy and reliability. The data elements that result from this stage of the process are the common highly important elements discussed in literature. Other elements such as vehicle maneuver, road functional class, and seating position, however, are placed under the second stage as it makes more sense if they are collected simultaneously with the road, person, and vehicle data elements.

The second stage includes the collection of datasets that are important but less of a priority than the core crash data elements. These include data from the crash investigation and will not require or benefit from the integration of database systems (except for junction type, road functional class, and speed limits). A key departure from the APRSO document is the proposed introduction of movement codes which will replace the crash type and impact type parameters. Using movement codes also replaces data elements such as maneuver and road obstacles. Movement codes are used in the MMUCC and CADaS data collection systems.

The third stage includes data elements that can be acquired by integrating the crash database with other database systems such as the road infrastructure database, and the licensing and vehicle registration database systems. This stage also includes linking to relevant external database systems such as the International Road Assessment Programme (iRAP). Table 5 shows the data elements found in each stage.

Table 5   Crash Data Elements for the Data Improvement Program

Core	Expanded	Integration
• Crash identifier (unique reference) • Crash date • Crash time • Crash location • Weather conditions • Light conditions • Crash severity • Vehicle type • Sex • Date of birth • Age • Type of road user (e.g. Driver, Passenger, Pedestrian) • Injury severity	• Movement Code* • Hit and run • Road functional class (e.g. national road, local road, etc.) • Speed limit • Road obstacles • Road surface conditions (e.g. dry, wet, etc.) • Junction type • Vehicle number • Person number • Occupant's linked vehicle number • Pedestrian's linked vehicle number • Safety equipment • Nationality • Suspected alcohol use • Alcohol test • Drug use • Seating position	• Traffic control at junction (e.g. traffic police, traffic light, etc.) • Road curve (e.g. tight curve, open curve, etc.) • Road segment grade (e.g. steep gradient or not) • Vehicle identification number/license plate • Vehicle make • Vehicle model • Vehicle registration number • Vehicle country of registration • Vehicle steering wheel position • Engine size • Vehicle model's year of manufacture • Vehicle special function • Person ID • Driving license issue date • Licensed vehicle category

Source: Asia–Pacific Road Safety Observatory, 2021.

The definitions and assigned values will still follow the APRSO task force document.[19] These are enumerated below for easier reference.

Crash identifier
- **Definition:** The unique identifier (e.g. a 10-digit number) within a given year that identifies a particular crash
- **Data improvement classification:** Core
- **Data type:** Numeric or character string
- **Comments:** The police usually assign this value, as they are responsible at the crash scene. Other systems may reference the incident using this number.

Crash date
- **Definition:** The date (day, month, and year) when the crash occurred
- **Data improvement classification:** Core
- **Data type:** Numeric (DD/MM/YYYY)
- **Comments:** If a part of the crash date is unknown, the respective places are filled in with 99 (for day and month). The absence of data for year should result in an edit check. Ths is important for seasonal comparisons, time series analyses, management/ administration, evaluation, and linkage.

Crash time
- **Definition:** The time at which the crash occurred, using the 24 hour-clock format (00.00–23:59).
- **Data improvement classification:** Core
- **Data type:** Numeric (HH:MM)
- **Comments:** Midnight is defined as 00:00 and represents the beginning of a new day. Variable allows for analyses of different time periods.

Crash location
- **Definition:** The exact location at which the crash occurred. Optimum definition is route name and GPS/ GIS coordinates if there is a linear referencing system, or other mechanisms that can relate geographic

19   APRSO Task Force Report on Crash Data Systems. Unpublished.

coordinates to specific locations in road inventory and other files. The minimum requirement for documentation of crash location is the street name, reference point, and distance and direction from reference point.

- **Data improvement classification:** Core
- **Data type:** Character string to support latitude/longitude coordinates, linear referencing method, or link node system.
- **Comments:** This is critical for problem identification, prevention programs, engineering evaluations, and mapping and linkage purposes.

Weather conditions

- **Definition:** Prevailing atmospheric conditions at the crash location, at the time of the crash.
- **Data improvement classification:** Core
- **Data type:** Numeric
- **Data values:** Not applicable (N/A)
  1 **Clear** (no hindrance from weather; no condensation or intense movement of air; clear and cloudy sky included)
  2 **Rain** (heavy or light)
  3 **Snow**
  4 **Fog, mist or smoke**
  5 **Sleet, hail**
  6 **Severe winds** (presence of winds deemed to have an adverse effect on driving conditions)
  8 **Other weather condition**
  9 **Unknown weather condition**
- **Comments:** This allows for the identification of the impact of weather conditions on road safety, which is important for engineering evaluations and prevention programs.

Light conditions

- **Definition:** The level of natural and artificial light at the crash location, at the time of the crash.
- **Data type:** Numeric
- **Data improvement classification:** Core
- **Data values:** Not applicable (N/A)
  1 **Daylight:** Natural lighting during daytime.
  2 **Twilight:** Natural lighting during dusk or dawn. Residual category covering cases where daylight conditions were very poor.
  3 **Darkness:** No natural lighting, no artificial lighting
  4 **Dark with streetlights unlit:** Streetlights exist at the crash location but are unlit.
  5 **Dark with streetlights lit:** Streetlights exist at the crash location and are lit.
  6 **Dark with streetlights unknown if lit or unlit:** Streetlights exist at the crash location, but it is unknown if they are lit or unlit.
  9 **Unknown:** Light conditions at time of crash unknown
- **Comments:** Information about the presence of lighting is an important element in the analysis of spot location or network and in determining the effects of road illumination on nighttime crashes to guide future measures.

Crash severity

- **Definition:** Describes the severity of the road crash, based on the most severe injury of any person involved.
- **Data improvement classification:** Core
- **Data type:** Numeric
- **Data values:** Not applicable (N/A)
  1 **Fatal:** At least one person was killed immediately or died within 30 days because of the road crash.

2   **Serious/severe injury:** At least one person was hospitalized for at least 24 hours because of injuries sustained in the crash, while no one was killed. MiniCADaS proposes MAIS3+.[20]

3   **Slight/minor injury:** At least one of the participants in the crash was hospitalized less than 24 hours or no participant was hospitalized, seriously injured, or killed.

- **Comments:** This provides a quick reference to the crash severity, summarizing the data from individual personal injury records of the crash. It facilitates analysis by crash severity level. Several crash-related variables can be derived from the collected data, including number of vehicles involved, number of motorized vehicles involved, number of nonmotorized vehicles involved, number of fatalities, number of non-fatal injuries, and day of the week. These variables provide information without the user having to go back to individual records. Depending on the type of reports generated, deriving these data elements can save time and effort.

Type of roadway

- **Definition:** Describes the type of road, whether the road has two directions of travel, and whether the carriageway is physically divided. For crashes occurring at junctions, where the crash cannot be clearly allocated to one road, the road where the vehicle with priority was moving is indicated.
- **Data improvement classification:** Expanded
- **Data type:** Numeric
- **Data values:** Not applicable (N/A)
  1   **Motorway/freeway:** Road with separate carriageways for traffic in two directions, physically separated by a dividing strip not intended for traffic; road has no crossings at the same level with any other road, railway or tramway track, or footpath; road is sign-posted as a motorway and reserved for specified categories of motor vehicles.
  2   **Express road:** Road with traffic in two directions, carriageways not normally separated; accessible only from interchanges or controlled junctions; road is sign-posted as an express road and reserved for specified categories of motor vehicles; stopping and parking on the running carriageway are prohibited.
  3   **Urban road, two-way:** Road within the boundaries of a built-up area, with sign-posted entries and exits); single, undivided street with traffic in two directions, allowing relatively lower speeds (often up to 50 kilometers per hour [kph]) or unrestricted traffic; road has one or more lanes, which may or may not be marked.
  4   **Urban road, one-way:** Road within the boundaries of a built-up area, with sign-posted entries and exits; single, undivided street with traffic going in one direction and at relatively lower speeds (often up to 50 kph).
  5   **Road outside a built-up area:** Road outside the boundaries of a built-up area, with sign-posted entries and exits.
  6   **Restricted road:** A roadway with restricted access to public traffic; includes cul-de-sacs, driveways, lanes, and private roads.
  8   **Other:** Roadway of a type other than those listed above.
  9   **Unknown:** Not known where the incident occurred.
- **Comments:** This is important for comparing the crash rates of roads with similar design characteristics and for conducting comparative analyses between motorway and non-motorway roads.

Road functional class

- **Definition:** Describes the character of service or function of the road where the first harmful event took place. For crashes occurring at junctions, where the crash cannot be clearly allocated to one road, the road where the vehicle with priority was moving is indicated.
- **Data improvement classification:** Expanded

---

[20]   MAIS3+ is the Abbreviated Injury Scale (AIS) severity score applied in the United Kingdom. It is an ordinal scale of 1 to 6 (1 indicating a minor injury and 6 being maximal). A casualty that sustains an injury with a score of 3 or higher on the AIS is classified as clinically seriously injured (MAIS3+).

- **Data type:** Numeric
- **Data values:** Not applicable (N/A)
  1 **Principal arterial (transit):** Roads serving long distance and mainly interurban movements. Includes motorways (urban or rural) and express roads. Principal arterials may cross through urban areas, serving suburban movements. The traffic is characterized by high speeds and full or partial access control (interchanges or junctions controlled by traffic lights). Other roads leading to a principal arterial are connected to it through side collector roads.
  2 **Secondary arterial:** Arterial roads connected to principal arterials through interchanges or traffic light controlled junctions supporting and completing the urban arterial network; serving middle distance movements but not crossing through neighborhoods. Full or partial access control is not mandatory.
  3 **Collector:** Unlike arterials, collectors cross urban areas (neighborhoods) and collect or distribute the traffic to/from local roads; collectors also distribute traffic leading to secondary or principal arterials.
  4 **Local:** Roads used for direct access to various land uses (private property, commercial areas etc.); low service speeds are not designed to serve interstate or suburban movements.

Road surface conditions
- **Definition:** The condition of the road surface at the time and place of the crash.
- **Data improvement classification:** Expanded
- **Data type:** Numeric
- **Data values:** Not applicable (N/A)
  1 **Dry:** Dry and clean road surface.
  2 **Snow, frost, ice:** Snow, frost or ice on the road.
  3 **Slippery:** Slippery road surface due to sand, gravel, mud, leaves, or oil on the road; does not include snow, frost, ice or wet road surface.
  4 **Wet, damp:** Wet road surface; does not include flooding.
  5 **Flood:** Still or moving water on the road.
  6 **Other:** Other road surface conditions not mentioned above.
  9 **Unknown:** Road surface conditions were unknown.
- **Comments:** This is important for the identification of high wet-surface crash locations, engineering evaluation, and prevention measures.

Speed limit
- **Definition:** The legal speed limit at the location of the crash.
- **Data improvement classification:** Expanded
- **Data type:** Numeric
- **Data values:** Not applicable (N/A)
  nnn: The legal speed limit as provided by road signs or by the country's traffic laws for each road category, in kph.
- **Unknown:** The speed limit at the crash location is unknown.
- **Comments:** For crashes occurring at junctions, where the crash cannot be clearly allocated on one road, the speed limit for the road where the vehicle with priority was moving is indicated.

Road obstacles
- **Definition:** The presence of any person or object, which obstructed the movement of the vehicles on the road. This includes any animals standing or moving (either hit or not), and any objects not meant to be on the road, but does not include pedestrians or vehicles (parked or moving) or obstacles on the side of the carriageway (e.g. poles, trees, etc.).
- **Data improvement classification:** Expanded
- **Data type:** Numeric

- **Data values:** Not applicable (N/A)
    1. **Yes:** Road obstacle present at the crash site.
    2. **No:** No road obstacle present at the crash site.
    9. **Unknown:** Unknown presence of any road obstacles at the crash site. Countries where a large proportion of the road network is unpaved may wish to include the variable 'road surface type' to allow for analysis of crash rates by road surface type.

Junction type

- **Definition:** Indicates whether the crash occurred at a junction (two or more roads intersecting) and defines the type of the junction. In at-grade junctions, all roads intersect at the same level. In not-at-grade junctions, roads do not intersect at the same level.
- **Data improvement classification:** Expanded
- **Data type:** Numeric
- **Data values:** Not applicable (N/A)
    1. **At-grade, crossroad:** Road intersection with four arms
    2. **At-grade, roundabout:** Circular road
    3. **At-grade, T or staggered junction:** Road intersection with three arms; includes T-intersections and intersections with an acute angle.
    4. **At-grade, multiple junction:** Junction with more than four arms (excluding roundabouts).
    5. **At-grade, other:** Other at-grade junction type not described above
    6. **Not at grade:** Junction includes roads that do not intersect at the same level
    7. **Not at junction:** The crash has occurred at a distance greater than 20 meters from a junction.
    9. **Unknown:** The crash location relative to a junction is unknown
- **Comments:** Crashes occurring within 20 meters of a junction are considered as crashes at a junction. This is important for site-specific studies and the identification of appropriate engineering countermeasures.

Traffic control at junction

- **Definition:** Type of traffic control at the junction where crash occurred; applies only to crashes that occur at a junction.
- **Data improvement classification:** Integration
- **Data type:** Numeric
- **Data values:** Not applicable (N/A)
    1. **Authorized person:** Police officer or traffic warden at intersection controls the traffic; applicable even if traffic signals or other junction control systems are present.
    2. **Stop sign:** Priority is determined by stop sign(s).
    3. **Give-way sign or markings:** Give-way sign or markings determine priority.
    4. **Other traffic signs:** Priority is determined by traffic sign(s) other than "stop," "give way" or markings.
    5. **Automatic traffic signal (working):** Priority is determined by a traffic signal that was working at the time of the crash.
    6. **Automatic traffic signal (out of order):** A traffic signal is present but out of order at the time of crash.
    7. **Uncontrolled:** The junction is not controlled by an authorized person, traffic signs, markings, automatic traffic signals or other means.
    8. **Other:** The junction is controlled by means other than an authorized person, signs, markings or automatic traffic signals.
- **Comments:** If more than one value is applicable, (e.g. traffic signs and automatic traffic signals), record all that apply.

Road curve

- **Definition:** Indicates whether the crash occurred inside a curve, and what type of curve
- **Data improvement classification:** Integration
- **Data type:** Numeric
- **Data values:** Not applicable (N/A)
  1 **Tight curve:** The crash occurred inside a road curve that was tight (based on the judgment of the police officer).
  2 **Open curve:** The crash occurred inside a road curve that was open (based on the judgment of the police officer).
  3 **No curve:** The crash did not occur inside a road curve.
  9 **Unknown:** It is not defined whether the crash occurred inside a road curve.
- **Comments:** This is useful for the identification and diagnosis of high-crash locations, and for guiding changes to road design, speed limits, etc.

Road segment grade

- **Definition:** Indicates whether the crash occurred on a road segment with a steep gradient
- **Data improvement classification:** Integration
- **Data type:** Numeric
- **Data values:** Not applicable (N/A)
  1 **Yes:** The crash occurred at a road segment with a high grade.
  2 **No:** The crash did not occur at a road segment with a high grade.
  9 **Unknown:** It is not defined whether the crash occurred at a road segment with a high grade.
- **Comments:** This is useful for the identification and diagnosis of high-crash locations, and for guiding changes to road design, speed limits, etc.

Vehicle number

- **Definition:** Unique number on assigned to identify each vehicle involved in the crash
- **Data improvement classification:** Expanded
- **Data type:** Numeric, sequential number
- **Comments:** This allows the vehicle record to be cross-referenced with the crash record and person records.

Vehicle identification number

- **Definition:** Unique vehicle number attached to the engine compartment of the vehicle by the manufacturer to identify each vehicle involved in the crash
- **Data improvement classification:** Integration
- **Data type:** Numeric, sequential number
- **Comments:** This allows the vehicle record to be cross-referenced with the registration and person records.

Vehicle registration number

- **Definition**: Unique vehicle registration number appearing on the number plate and registration documents.
- **Data improvement classification:** Integration
- **Data type:** numeric, sequential number
- **Comments:** This allows cross-referencing with the vehicle identification number and identification.

Country of vehicle's registration

- **Definition:** Identifies the country where the vehicle is registered
- **Data improvement classification:** Integration
- **Data type:** Character string

Vehicle type
- **Definition:** The type of vehicle involved in the crash
- **Data improvement classification:** Core
- **Data type:** Numeric
- **Data values:** Not applicable (N/A)
    1 **Bicycle:** Road vehicle with two or more wheels, generally propelled solely by the energy of the person on the vehicle by means of a pedal system, lever or handle
    2 **Animal-powered vehicle:** Road vehicle with two or more wheels generally propelled solely by the energy of animals drawing it
    3 **Other non-motor vehicle:** Other vehicle without engine not included in the list above.
    4 **Two/three-wheel motor vehicle:** Two- or three-wheeled road motor vehicle (includes mopeds, motorcycles, tricycles and all-terrain vehicles)
    5 **Passenger car:** Road motor vehicle other than a two- or three-wheeled vehicle, intended to carry passengers and designed to seat no more than nine people (driver included).
    6 **Bus/coach/trolley:** Passenger-carrying vehicle, most commonly used for public transport, inter-urban movements, and tourist trips; seats more than nine persons and includes vehicles connected to electric conductors and which are not rail-borne.
    7 **Light goods vehicle (<3.5 t):** Smaller (by weight) motor vehicle designed exclusively or primarily for the transport of goods
    8 **Heavy goods vehicle (≥3.5 t):** Larger (by weight) motor vehicle designed exclusively or primarily for the transport of goods
    9 **Other motor vehicle:** Other vehicle not powered by an engine and not included in the two previous lists of values.
    10 **Unknown:** The type of the vehicle is unknown or it was not stated.
- **Comments:** This allows for analysis of crash risk by vehicle type and road user type. It is important for the evaluation of countermeasures designed for specific vehicles or the protection of specific road users.

Vehicle make
- **Definition:** Indicates the make (distinctive name) assigned by the motor vehicle manufacturer
- **Data improvement classification:** Integration
- **Data type:** Character string. Alternatively, a list of motor vehicle makes can be created, with a code corresponding to each make. Such a list allows for more consistent and reliable recording, as well as easier data interpretation.
- **Comments:** This allows for crash analyses related to various motor vehicle makes.

Vehicle model
- **Definition:** The code assigned by the manufacturer to denote a family of motor vehicles (within a make) that have a degree of similarity in construction
- **Data improvement classification:** Integration
- **Data type:** Character string. Alternatively, a list of motor vehicle models can be created, with a code corresponding to each model. Such a list allows for more consistent and reliable recording, as well as easier data interpretation.
- **Comments:** Record the name of the model as referred to in the country where the crash occurred. This allows for crash analyses related to various motor vehicle models.

Vehicle model year
- **Definition:** The year assigned to a motor vehicle by the manufacturer.
- **Data improvement classification:** Integration

- **Data type:** Numeric (YYYY)
- **Comments:** This can be obtained from vehicle registration and is important in identifying motor vehicle model year for evaluation, research, and crash comparison purposes.

Engine size

- **Definition:** The size of the vehicle's engine is recorded in cubic centimeters
- **Data improvement classification:** Integration
- **Data type:** Numeric
- **Data values:** Not applicable (N/A)
    - **nnnn: Size of engine**
    - **9999: Unk**nown engine size
- **Comments:** This is important for identifying the impact of motor vehicle power on crash risk.

Vehicle special function

- **Definition:** The type of special function being served by this vehicle regardless of whether the function is marked on the vehicle
- **Data improvement classification:** Integration
- **Data type:** Numeric
- **Data values:** Not applicable (N/A)
    1 **No special function:** No special function of the vehicle
    2 **Taxi:** Licensed passenger car for hire with driver, without predetermined routes
    3 **Vehicle used as bus:** Passenger road motor vehicle used for the transport of people
    4 **Police/military:** Motor vehicle used for police/military purposes
    5 **Emergency vehicle:** Motor vehicle used for emergency purposes, including ambulances, fire-service vehicles, etc.
    8 **Other:** Other special functions not mentioned above.
    9 **Unknown:** It was not possible to record a special function.
- **Comments:** This helps to evaluate the crash involvement of vehicles based on their special uses.

Vehicle steering wheel position

- **Definition:** Identifies whether the vehicle is left-hand drive or right-hand drive.
- **Data improvement classification:** Integration
- **Data type:** Numeric
- **Data values: Not applicable (N/A)**
    1 **Left-hand drive**: Steering wheel is located at the left side of the vehicle.
    2 **Right-hand drive:** Steering wheel is located at the right side of the vehicle.
    9 **Unknown:** Location of the steering wheel in the vehicle is unknown or not recorded.
- **Comments:** This allows for the analysis of crash risk in countries where both left-hand drive and right-hand drive vehicles are used.

Person number

- **Definition:** Number assigned to uniquely identify each person involved in the crash
- **Data improvement classification:** Expanded
- **Data type:** Numeric (two-digit number, nn)
- **Comments:** The persons related to the first (presumed liable) vehicle will be recorded first. Within a specific vehicle, the driver will be recorded first, followed by the passengers. This allows the person record to be cross-referenced with the crash, road, and vehicle records to establish a unique linkage with the crash ID and the vehicle number.

Occupant's vehicle number

- **Definition:** The unique number assigned for this crash to the motor vehicle in which the person was an occupant
- **Data improvement classification:** Expanded
- **Data type:** Numeric (two-digit number, nn)
- **Comments:** This allows the person record to be cross-referenced with the vehicle records, linking the persons to the motor vehicle in which they were traveling.

Pedestrian's linked vehicle number

- **Definition:** The unique number assigned for this crash to the motor vehicle that collided with this person. The vehicle number assigned to the motor vehicle that collided with this person.
- **Data improvement classification:** Expanded
- **Data type:** Numeric (two-digit number, nn, from V1)
- **Comments:** This allows the person record to be cross-referenced with the vehicle records, linking the person to the motor vehicle that struck him or her.

Date of birth

- **Definition:** Indicates the date of birth of the person involved in the crash.
- **Data improvement classification:** Core
- **Data type:** Numeric (date format – DD/MM/YYYY, 99/99/9999 if birth date unknown)
- **Comments:** This allows the calculation of the person's age, which is important for the analysis of crash risk by age group and the assessment of the effectiveness of occupant protection systems by age group. This provides a key variable for linkage with records in other databases.

Sex

- **Definition:** Indicates the sex of the person involved in the crash.
- **Data improvement classification:** Core
- **Data type:** Numeric
- **Data values:** Not applicable (N/A)
    1 **Male:** Based on identification documents/personal ID number or as determined by the police
    2 **Female:** Based on identification documents/personal ID number or as determined by the police
    9 **Unknown:** Sex could not be determined (police unable to trace person, not specified).
- **Comments:** This is important for the analysis of crash risk by sex and the evaluation of the effect of a person's sex on occupant protection systems and motor vehicle design characteristics.

Type of road user

- **Definition:** Indicates the role of each person at the time of the crash
- **Data improvement classification:** Core
- **Data type:** Numeric
- **Data values:** Not applicable (N/A)
    1 **Driver:** Driver or operator of motorized or nonmotorized vehicle; includes cyclists and persons pulling a rickshaw or riding an animal
    2 **Passenger:** Person in a vehicle, who is not the driver; includes person in the act of boarding, alighting from a vehicle, or sitting/standing in the vehicle.
    3 **Pedestrian:** Person on foot, pushing or holding a bicycle, pram or a pushchair, leading or herding an animal, riding a toy cycle, on roller skates, skateboard or skis; excludes persons in the act of boarding or alighting from a vehicle
    8 **Other:** Person involved in the crash who is not of any type listed above
    9 **Unknown:** It is not known what role the person played in the crash.
- **Comments:** This allows for the analysis of crash risk by road user type, in combination with vehicle type (V2), and is important for the evaluation of countermeasures designed to protect specific road users.

Seating position
- **Definition:** The location of the person in the vehicle at the time of the crash.
- **Data improvement classification:** Expanded
- **Data type:** Numeric
- **Subfield: Row**
- **Data values:** Not applicable (N/A)
  - 1 **Front**
  - 2 **Rear**
  - 3 **Not applicable** (e.g. riding on motor vehicle exterior)
  - 8 **Other**
  - 9 **Unknown**
- **Subfield: Seat**
- **Data values:** Not applicable (N/A)
  - 1 **Left**
  - 2 **Middle**
  - 3 **Right**
  - 4 **Not applicable** (e.g. riding on motor vehicle exterior)
  - 8 **Other**
  - 9 **Unknown**
- **Comments:** This is important for the full evaluation of occupant protection programs.

Injury severity
- **Definition:** The level of injury severity for a person involved in the crash
- **Data improvement classification:** Core
- **Data type:** Numeric
- **Data values:** Not applicable (N/A)
  - 1 **Fatal injury:** Person was killed immediately or died within 30 days as a result of the crash
  - 2 **Serious/severe injury:** Person was hospitalized for at least 24 hours because of injuries sustained in the crash.
  - 3 **Slight/minor injury:** Person was injured and hospitalized for less than 24 hours or not hospitalized; MAIS3+ in MiniCadas
  - 4 **No injury:** Person was not injured.
  - 9 **Unknown:** Injury severity was not recorded or is unknown.
- **Comment:** This is important for injury outcome analysis, evaluation, and appropriate classification of crash severity (PD1), as well for establishing a linkage with records in other databases.

Safety equipment
- **Definition:** Describes the use of occupant restraints, or helmet use by a motorcyclist or bicyclist.
- **Data improvement classification:** Expanded
- **Data type:** Numeric
- **Subfield: Occupant restraints**
- **Data values:** Not applicable (N/A)
  - 1 **Seatbelt available, used**
  - 2 **Seatbelt available, not used**
  - 3 **Seatbelt not available**
  - 4 **Child restraint system available, used**
  - 5 **Child restraint system available, not used**
  - 6 **Child restraint system not available**
  - 7 **Not applicable:** No occupant restraints could be used on the specific vehicle such as in agricultural tractors.

8 **Other restraints used**

9 **Unknown:** Not known if occupant restraints were in use at the time of the crash.

10 **No restraints used**

- **Subfield: Helmet use**
- **Data values:** Not applicable (N/A)

1 **Helmet worn**

2 **Helmet not worn**

3 **Not applicable** (e.g. person was a pedestrian or car occupant)

9 **Unknown**

- **Comments:** Information on the availability and use of occupant restraint systems and helmets is important for evaluating the effect of such safety equipment on injury outcomes.

Suspected alcohol use

- **Definition:** Law enforcement officer suspects that the person involved in the crash has consumed alcohol.
- **Data improvement classification:** Expanded
- **Data type:** Numeric
- **Data values:** Not applicable (N/A)

1 **No**

2 **Yes**

3 **Not applicable** (e.g. if the person is not the driver of motorized vehicle)

9 **Unknown**

Alcohol test

- **Definition:** Describes alcohol test status, type, and result.
- **Data improvement classification:** Expanded
- **Data type:** Numeric
- **Subfield: Test status**
- **Data values:** Not applicable (N/A)

1 **Test not given**

2 **Test refused**

3 **Test given**

9 **Unknown if tested**

- **Subfield: Test type**
- **Data values:** Not applicable (N/A)

1 **Blood**

2 **Breath**

3 **Urine**

8 **Other**

9 **Test type unknown**

- **Subfield: Test result**
- **Data values**

1 **Pending**

9 **Result unknown**

- **Comments:** Alcohol-related crashes are a major road safety problem. Information on alcohol involvement in crashes facilitates the evaluation of programs to reduce drunk driving.

Drug use
- **Definition:** Indication of suspicion or evidence that the person involved in the crash has used illegal drugs.
- **Data improvement classification:** Expanded
- **Data type:** Numeric
- **Data values:** Not applicable (N/A)
  1 **No suspicion or evidence of drug use**
  2 **Suspicion of drug use**
  3 **Evidence of drug use** (further subfields can specify test type and values)
  4 **Not applicable** (e.g. if the person is not the driver of the motorized vehicle)
  9 **Unknown**

Driving license issue date
- **Definition:** Indicates the date (month and year) of issue of the person's first driving license, provisional or full, pertaining to the vehicle he or she was driving.
- **Data improvement classification:** Integration
- **Data type:** Numeric (MM/YYYY)
- **Data values:** Not applicable (N/A)
- **Value (MM/YYYY)**
  1 **Never issued a driving license**
  9 **Date of issue of first license unknown**
- **Comments:** This allows the calculation of the number of years of driving experience at the time of crash.

Licensed vehicle category
- **Definition:** Whether the driving license allowed the driver to operate the vehicle he or she was operating.
- **Data improvement classification:** Integration
- **Data type:** Numeric
- **Data values:** Not applicable (N/A)
  1 **Yes**
  2 **No**
  9 **Unknown**

Age
- **Definition:** The age in years of the person involved in the crash
- **Data improvement classification:** Core
- **Data type:** Numeric
- **Comments:** Derived from the date of birth and crash date, this is important for the analysis of crash risk by age group, and the assessment of the effectiveness of countermeasures by age group.

Driver Nationality
- **Definition:** The nationality of the driver of the vehicle.
- **Data improvement classification:** Expanded
- **Data type:** Character string

Hit and run
- **Definition:** The behavior of a driver of a vehicle who is involved in a collision with another vehicle, property, or human being, who knowingly fails to stop to give his or her name, license number, and other information as required by statute to the injured party, a witness, or law enforcement officers.
- **Data improvement classification:** Expanded
- **Data type:** Yes or No
- **Comments**: Information is captured when there is more than one vehicle involved in the crash but not all vehicles' data are available.

Recommendations on the Use of Movement Codes

A more detailed system of effectively classifying crash types should be implemented. This system can be most appropriately illustrated in the form of movement codes. A movement code is a system of classifying crashes using standard and predefined diagrams based on road users and their movements and activities leading to a crash. It is also referred to as Definition for Coding Accidents in Australia.[21] There are code systems that are sophisticated, detailed, and covers primary crash types which are subdivided into secondary and more specific types. For example, a primary crash type would be "Hit Pedestrian" and the secondary type is "Hit Pedestrian on a Crossing." An example of a sophisticated coding system is the set of movement codes in New Zealand which have at least 50 movement codes (Figure 8).

A simpler coding system is used in New Jersey, US, that only has 18 movement codes, as presented in the State of New Jersey Police Crash Investigation Report (Figure 9).

Movement codes can provide a more detailed description of the crash which is crucial for the development of effective road treatments. They can replace crash data elements such as crash and impact types, vehicle, and pedestrian maneuver. Visuals, more than text descriptions, make it easier for data gatherers to assign a crash type, which can significantly result in better quality and consistent data.

---

21   B. Turner et al. 2015. *Guide to Road Safety Part 8: Treatment of Crash Locations*. Australia: Austroads.

Figure 8   Movement Codes in New Zealand

	TYPE	A	B	C	D	E	F	G	O
A	OVERTAKING AND LANE CHANGE	PULLING OUT OR CHANGING LANE TO RIGHT	HEAD ON	CUTTING IN OR CHANGING LANE TO LEFT	LOST CONTROL (OVERTAKEN VECHICLE)	SIDE ROAD	LOST CONTROL (OVERTAKEN VECHICLE)	WEAVING IN HEAVY TRAFFIC	OTHER
B	HEAD ON	ON STRAIGHT	CUTTING CORNER	SWINGING WIDE	BOTH OR UNKNOWN	LOST CONTROL ON STRAIGHT	LOST CONTROL ON CURVE		OTHER
C	LOST CONTROL OR OFF ROAD (STRAIGHT ROADS)	OUT OF CONTROL ON ROADWAY	OFF ROADWAY TO LEFT	OFF ROADWAY TO RIGHT					OTHER
D	CORNERING	LOST CONTROL TURNING RIGHT	LOST CONTROL TURNING LEFT	MISSED INTER SECTION OR END OF ROAD					OTHER
E	COLLISION WITH OBSTRUCTION	PARKED VEHICLE	CRASH OR BROKEN DOWN	NON VEHICULAR OBSTRUCTIONS (INCLUDING ANIMALS)	WORKMANS VEHICLE	OPENING DOOR			OTHER
F	REAR END	SLOWER VEHICLE	CROSS TRAFFIC	PEDESTRIAN	QUEUE	SIGNALS	OTHER		OTHER
G	TURNING VERSUS SAME DIRECTION	REAR OF LEFT TURNING VECHICLE	LEFT TURN SIDE SIDE SWIPE	STOPPED OR TURNING FROM LEFT SIDE	NEAR CENTRE LINE	OVERTAKING VEHICLE	TWO TURNING		OTHER
H	CROSSING (NO TURNS)	RIGHT ANGLE (70° TO 110°)							OTHER
J	CROSSING (VEHICLE TURNING)	RIGHT TURN RIGHT SIDE	OPPOSING RIGHT TURNS	TWO TURNING					OTHER
K	MERGING	LEFT TURN IN	RIGHT TURN IN	TWO TURNING					OTHER
L	RIGHT TURN AGAINST	STOPPED WAITING TO TURN	MAKING TURN						OTHER
M	MANEUVERING	PARKING OR LEAVING	"U" TURN	"U" TURN	DRIVEWAY MANUEVER	ENTERING OR LEAVING FROM OPPOSITE SIDE	ENTERING OR LEAVING FROM SAME SIDE	REVERSING ALONG ROAD	OTHER
N	PEDESTRIANS CROSSING ROAD	LEFT SIDE	RIGHT SIDE	LEFT TURN LEFT SIDE	RIGHT TURN RIGHT SIDE	LEFT TURN RIGHT SIDE	RIGHT TURN LEFT SIDE	MANOEUVRING VEHICLE	OTHER
P	PEDESTRIANS OTHER	WALKING WITH TRAFFIC	WALKING FACING TRAFFIC	WALKING ON FOORPATH	CHILD PLAYING (INCLUDING TRICYCLE)	ATTENDING TO VEHICLE	ENTERING OR LEAVING VEHICLE		OTHER
Q	MISCELLANEOUS	FELL WHILE BOARDING OR ALIGHTING	FELL FROM MOVING VECHICLE	TRAIN	PARKED VEHICLE RAN AWAY	EQUESTRIAN	FELL INSIDE VEHICLE	TRAILER OR LOAD	OTHER

Source: Ausroads, 2015.

Figure 9   Movement Codes in New Jersey

Crash Type Diagrams

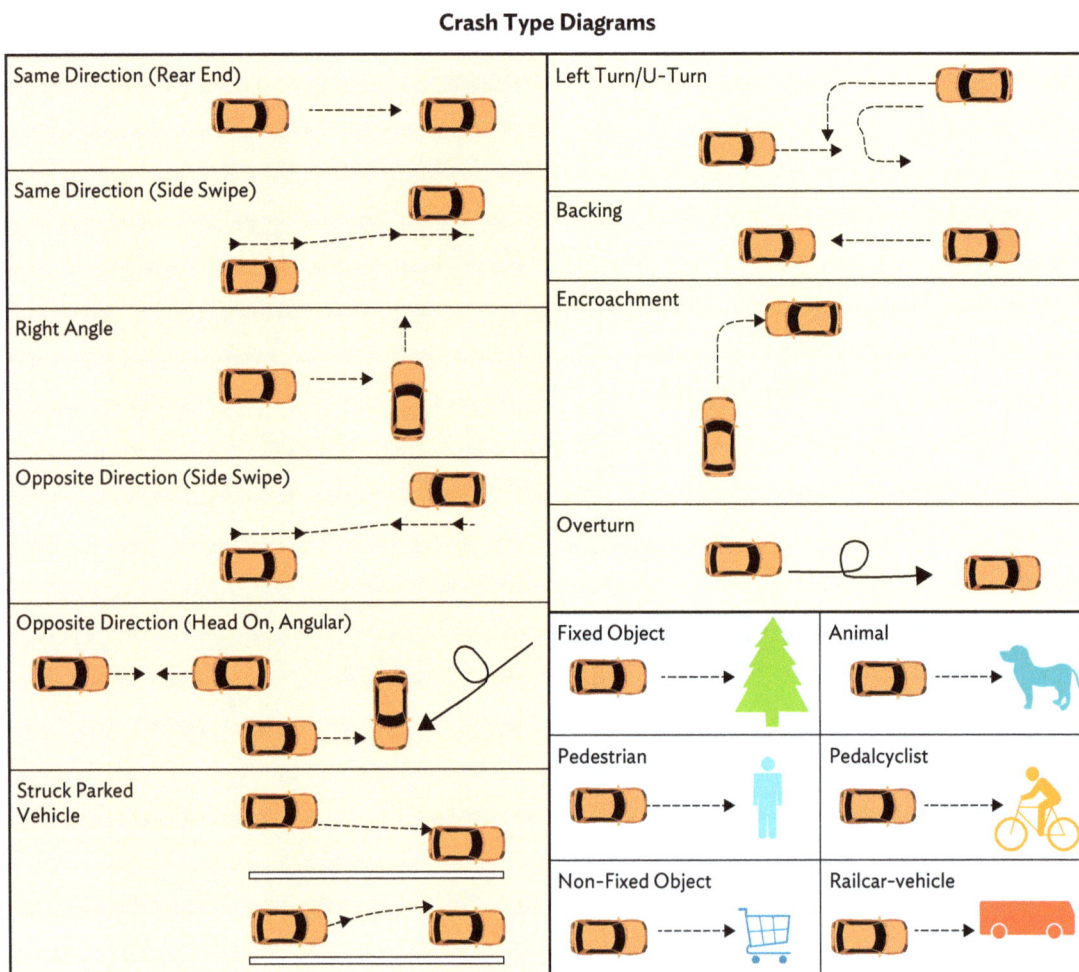

Source: State of New Jersey.

4. Crash Data Elements at the Regional Level

Literature Review

In a regional scope, crash data elements that countries may share to the APRSO could be limited by different factors. These include privacy and confidentiality concerns; technological and resource limitations (e.g. lack of a national database system); and costs in collecting and sharing data. Data shared with the observatory should be relevant and useful for cross-country analysis and should be aligned with the strategic goals and priorities of the observatory. Not all crash data elements are needed at the regional level, as seen in the practice of regional institutions collecting data from different countries.

Community Database on Accidents on the Roads in Europe

The EU's Community Database on Accidents on the Roads in Europe (CARE) aims to collect detailed data on crashes from each European Union (EU) member country. CADaS was developed so that data reporting can be standardized and comparisons can be made for each country.[22] Sample analytics generated through CARE are road deaths per million inhabitants, among others (Figure 10).

MiniCADaS

While most types of analysis are aggregate and summary in nature, each country in the EU still submits and shares mandatory crash data elements. This list of mandatory data elements is called MiniCADaS. As of 2019, MiniCADaS comprises 24 crash data elements, including incident, road, vehicle, and person details. MiniCADaS is being proposed for adoption by the Ibero-American Road Safety Observatory and the African Road Safety Observatory.

International Road Traffic Safety Data and Analysis Group

The International Road Traffic Safety Data and Analysis Group (IRTAD) of the International Transport Forum collects aggregated road safety data from its member countries using a standardized format and common data definitions derived from the IRTAD database. These include fatality and injury crash data by road type, road user, age, and gender. A sample country analysis is shown in Figure 11.

---

[22]   M. Villegas. 2011. *CARE Database.* https://www.unece.org/fileadmin/DAM/trans/doc/2011/wp6/ECE-TRANS-WP6-2011-pres08e.pdf.

Figure 10   Road Fatalities per Million Inhabitants in the European Union, 2019 and 2010

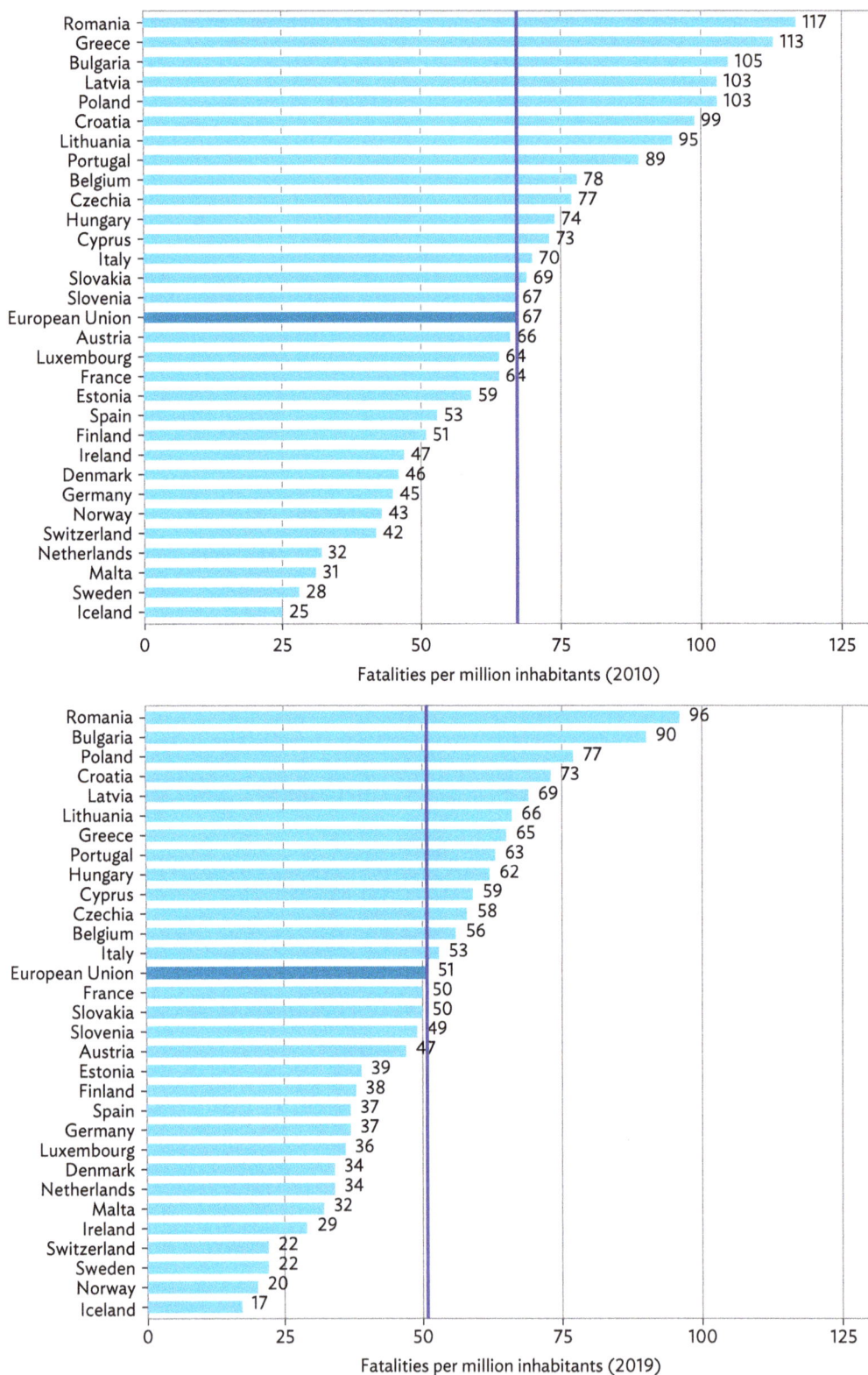

Fatalities per million inhabitants (2010)

Romania 117
Greece 113
Bulgaria 105
Latvia 103
Poland 103
Croatia 99
Lithuania 95
Portugal 89
Belgium 78
Czechia 77
Hungary 74
Cyprus 73
Italy 70
Slovakia 69
Slovenia 67
European Union 67
Austria 66
Luxembourg 64
France 64
Estonia 59
Spain 53
Finland 51
Ireland 47
Denmark 46
Germany 45
Norway 43
Switzerland 42
Netherlands 32
Malta 31
Sweden 28
Iceland 25

Fatalities per million inhabitants (2019)

Romania 96
Bulgaria 90
Poland 77
Croatia 73
Latvia 69
Lithuania 66
Greece 65
Portugal 63
Hungary 62
Cyprus 59
Czechia 58
Belgium 56
Italy 53
European Union 51
France 50
Slovakia 50
Slovenia 49
Austria 47
Estonia 39
Finland 38
Spain 37
Germany 37
Luxembourg 36
Denmark 34
Netherlands 34
Malta 32
Ireland 29
Switzerland 22
Sweden 22
Norway 20
Iceland 17

Source: Community Database on Accidents on the Roads in Europe, 2011.

Figure 11   Evolution of Road Fatalities per 100,000 Inhabitants, 2000–2017

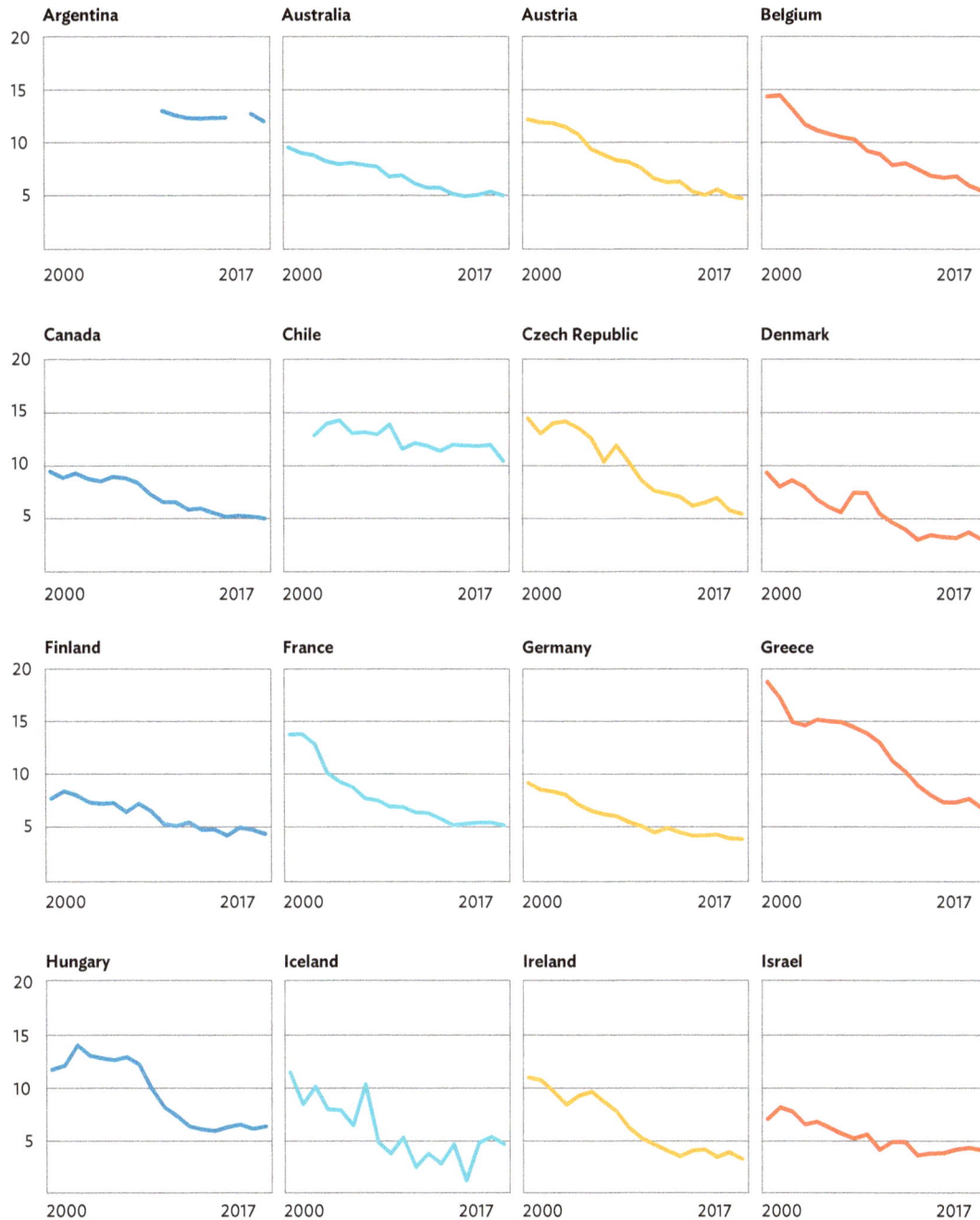

Source: International Transport Forum, 2019.

Recommended Crash Data Elements to be Collected by the Asia-Pacific Road Safety Observatory

Since the APRSO is in the initial stages of establishment and member countries are still in varying stages of setting up their own national crash database systems, it is recommended that data elements to be collected from each country be divided into three stages.

In the initial phase, it is proposed that the APRSO collect aggregated data of key crash data elements similar to the data elements collected by IRTAD. The main objective of the initial phase is to establish a baseline for the regional road safety situation and analyze patterns and trends among countries. This will also enable the APRSO to set initial strategic priorities and programs for road safety. IRTAD collects the number of fatalities and injuries, as well as the number of fatalities and injuries per road, vehicle type, gender, age, and road-user type. It is recommended that the APRSO collect the same aggregate data from its member countries, specifically the number of the following:

- fatalities and injuries per month;
- fatalities, hospitalized, and injured by road type;
- fatalities, hospitalized, and injured by vehicle type and age of person involved;
- fatalities, hospitalized, and injured by vehicle type;
- females/males killed at each age in yearly interval; and
- drivers/passengers/unknown, the seating position of passenger cars/goods/light goods/articulated, and non-articulated heavy goods killed.

To operationalize this and enable effective cross-country comparison, member countries must agree to standardize the definition of fatality and injury severities.

The APRSO can then collect more detailed data in the second phase. It can ask countries for disaggregated individual crash records once data can already be shared by the member countries. A key component of the second phase is the georeferencing of individual crash records. This will allow the APRSO to map out where crashes are happening in the region and identify high-risk locations. While the MiniCADaS requires 24 indicators, it is recommended that the APRSO initially collect individual crash records with these core data elements:

- crash identifier (unique reference);
- crash date;
- crash time;
- crash location;
- weather conditions;
- light conditions;
- crash severity;
- vehicle type;
- sex;
- date of birth;
- age;
- type of road user (e.g. driver, passenger, pedestrian); and
- injury severity.

The rationale is that numerous member countries are still developing their own systems. A small set of crash data elements for the APRSO ensures that data remain reliable which, in turn, enables effective cross-country comparison.

The final phase widens the list of data elements to be collected by the APRSO from member countries. The final list can be decided later on by the member countries depending on regional priorities and programs. Another option is to adopt the MiniCADaS in the final phase.

5. Safety Performance Indicators at the National Level

Safety Performance Indicators

To properly describe road safety and road conditions, the crash data must be augmented with other characteristics that describe and relate the crash data to various socioeconomic parameters and conditions that provide a context to the analysis. This enables and facilitates better analysis and presentation of the results, and in an international context enables cross-country comparisons.

A key subgroup of road safety indicators are the safety performance indicators (SPIs). In its broadest sense, SPIs are used to understand safety risks in the road environment that can lead to crash fatalities and severe injuries. SPIs can be used to monitor and evaluate the safety of roads and transport systems, transport operations, and infrastructure. They can be qualitative or quantitative while being directly related to crash occurrence, crash severity, and practical data collection methods. These criteria imply that while there is a multitude of data available, only a few SPIs can reliably and accurately determine the safety risk on the road. In this regard, SPIs are able to capture and monitor the progress of countries in meeting the voluntary global performance targets.

WHO discusses SPIs but emphasizes that coming up with a list of indicators would require a thorough review of current data and data collection practices.[23] This is especially true for the APRSO as a whole and the individual member countries. WHO has referenced previous experiences in Europe in enumerating the immediate outcome indicators. More specifically, WHO identified the incidence of drunk driving, speeding, seatbelt use, and child restraints.

The World Road Association or PIARC (2019), on the other hand, cited examples of non-crash data that can be used for analysis.[24] These include data on road inventory, traffic, exposure, attitude survey, and enforcement.

At the national level, the Global Road Safety Partnership (GRSP) has recently developed specific SPIs that are in line with the voluntary global performance targets.[25] *Towards the 12 Voluntary Global Targets for Road Safety* provides SPIs for speed, safety equipment, drunk driving, road infrastructure, vehicle standards, driver fatigue, and emergency care, along with other indicators (e.g., implementation indicators). However, some of these indicators require resources beyond the capacity of most member countries in the APRSO. These include conducting surveys and roadside observational studies. At the national level, simpler indicators that can be collected from existing institutions or processes are recommended.

---

23   WHO. 2010. Data Systems: *A Road Safety Manual for Decision-Makers and Practitioners*. https://www.who.int/roadsafety/projects/manuals/data/en/.

24   World Road Association. 2019. *Road Safety Manual - World Road Association (PIARC)* https://roadsafety.piarc.org/en.

25   Global Road Safety Partnership. 2020. *Towards the 12 Global Road Safety Performance Targets*. https://www.grsproadsafety.org/wp-content/uploads/Towards-the-12-Voluntary-Global-Targets-for-Road-Safety.pdf.

Recommendations for Safety Performance Indicators at the National Level

Following the voluntary global performance targets, it is recommended that member countries collect SPIs grouped under the following categories:
- speed;
- alcohol and drugs;
- safety equipment – cars;
- safety equipment – motorcycles;
- distracted driving;
- vehicles;
- roads; and
- post-crash response.

The following provides a brief discussion of these categories, their link to road safety, and proposed SPIs that countries can collect at the national level. A summary of national-level SPIs is provided in Table 6.

Speed

Speeding is a core road safety issue. As speed increases, the likelihood of a crash fatality and severe injury increases. By reducing the speed of vehicles, the crash rate[26] and crash fatality rate can be reduced.[27] According to the power model developed by Nilsson, a 5% cut in average speed can result in a 20% reduction in the number of fatal road crashes. Speeding is a major risk factor for road crash injuries, contributing to both crash risk and crash consequences.

Speeding occurs across different road users, road types, and times of day, so SPIs on speeding should consider these differences. The PIARC recommends the use of spot surveys in collecting speed data (footnote 24). Spot surveys are conducted in road corridors (not intersections) and speeds are collected for each direction of traffic. To collect data, roadside monitoring equipment, automated speed enforcement devices, and vehicle tracking or monitoring devices are needed.

WHO enumerates the types of speed data that can be collected at the country level, which could point to free-flow travel speeds, speed distribution, and speed variance (footnote 23). They are as follows:
- Number of fatalities where speed was a contributing factor.
- Number of fatalities as a result of speeding by road user type, age and sex of all involved in speeding crashes.
- Type of road, traffic volume, and speed limit of roads where speed crashes have occurred.

Considering the context of the Asia and the Pacific, countries have varying capacities for collecting data. Indirectly, they collect speed data through enforcement data such as the number of violations on the speed limit. Speed data can also be gleaned from crash data although countries face many issues in the collection of crash data. On the other hand, observational studies on speed might exist only as part of a larger study on transport or road infrastructure, and monitoring of speed data is not as widespread and common in the region. Given this, it is proposed that countries start off with indicators that are already collected from other datasets.

---

[26] Government of the United Kingdom, Department of Environment, Transport and the Regions. 2000. *New Directions in Speed Management – A Review of Policy*. London: Department of Environment, Transport and the Regions.
[27] T. Toroyan and M. Peden, eds. 2007. *Youth and Road Safety*. Geneva: WHO.

At the national level, the collection of indicators such as the number of speeding violations by road type and the number of fatalities and injuries caused by speeding must be improved. This will require countries not just to improve their crash database systems but to have clearly defined speed limit legislation and resources to collect speed data (e.g. speed guns). In the future, with the guidance of the APRSO, member countries can have more targeted data collection on speeds.

Drunk and Drug Driving

Alcohol and drugs impair the ability of road users to behave safely on the road. These impairments include the lack of awareness and clear sight, hampered decision-making skills, and delayed reactions, among others as seen in Figure 12. WHO lists the impact of alcohol on the body for different blood alcohol concentration (BAC) levels (footnote 23).

The effects are similar to those who use drugs, particularly the delayed reaction time and judgment, decreased hand–eye coordination, and reduced awareness and control. These effects are associated with the increased likelihood of road crash fatalities and severe injuries.

Given the clear link between alcohol and drug use and crash fatalities and severe injuries, indicators based on alcohol and drugs can be helpful in managing road safety issues. Similar with speed limits, robust information on drunk and drug driving is inadequate in many countries in Asia and the Pacific. Ideally, countries should be collecting the number of drivers testing above the legal alcohol limit, but collecting these data might be difficult especially for countries that are in the early stages of improving their road safety data. Alternatively, countries can use indicators such as the number and percentage of severe injuries and fatalities that are caused by one road user that has a BAC exceeding the legal limit, and the number and percentage of severe injuries and fatalities that are caused by one road user positive for drug use. These indicators can be collected through crash data.

Safety Equipment

Safety equipment for vehicles and motorcycles are crucial in protecting the body from severe injuries. Injuries to the head and neck are the main causes of death and severe injuries among motorcyclists. Helmet wearing is one way to protect motorcyclists from head injuries and consequently, fatalities. According to the Johns Hopkins School of Public Health, helmet wearing reduces the risk and severity of injuries by 72% and the fatality risk by 39%.[28] Seatbelt wearing reduces the risk of fatality by vehicle occupants by at least 40% while child restraints can protect children in vehicles by 71%.

In the Asian context where motorcycle use is prevalent, an indicator for helmet wearing is warranted. It is recommended that a helmet wearing rate indicator be used as not all countries in Asia and the Pacific have laws for wearing helmets. The GRSP improves on this indicator and suggests the use of approved standards to determine the percentage of motorcyclists appropriately wearing helmets. Similar to a straightforward indicator for helmets, the rates of use of seatbelts and child restraints are recommended indicators for the member countries.

---

28   Johns Hopkins School of Public Health. 2020. *Presentation on Risk Factors.*

Figure 12   **Effects of Different Blood Alcohol Concentration Levels on the Body**

BAC (g/100ml)	Effects on the Body
0.01–0.05	Increase in heart and respiration rates
	Decrease in various brain center functions
	Inconsistent effects on behavioral task performances
	Decrease in judgment and inhibitions
	Mild sense of elation, relaxation, and pleasure
0.06–0.10	Physiological sedation of nearly all systems
	Decreased attention and alertness, slowed reactions, impaired coordination, and reduced muscle strength
	Reduced ability to make rational decisions or exercise good judgment
	Increase in anxiety and depression
	Decrease in patience
0.10–0.15	Dramatic slowing of reactions
	Impairment of balance and movement
	Impairment of some visual functions
	Slurred speech
	Vomiting, especially if this BAC is reached rapidly
0.16–0.29	Severe sensory impairment, including reduced awareness of external stimulation
	Severe motor impairment, e.g., frequently staggering or falling
0.30–0.39	Nonresponsive stupor
	Loss of consciousness
	Anesthesia comparable to that for surgery
	Death (for many)
0.40 and greater	Unconsciousness
	Cessation of breathing
	Death, usually due to respiratory failure

BAC = blood alcohol concentration, g/100ml = grams of alcohol per 100 milliliters of blood.
Source: World Health Organization. 2010. Data systems: a road safety manual for decision-makers and practitioners. https://www.who.int/roadsafety/projects/manuals/data/en/.

Distracted Driving

With the rapid proliferation of mobile phone use, more and more countries observe that distracted driving results in fatalities and severe injuries. The Johns Hopkins School of Public Health notes that mobile phone use can prevent drivers from focusing their eyes, mind, and body on the road (footnote 28). This results in delayed reaction times and lack of vehicle control. It is believed that drivers using mobile phones are four times more likely to be involved in a crash, and the risks are not mitigated even if the driver is using a hands-free phone. Because of this emerging issue, indicators on distracted driving derived from enforcement and crash data are proposed.

Vehicles

The quality of vehicles is a key risk factor for road safety. Those who use unsafe vehicles are more vulnerable to severe injuries and fatalities in a crash. Vehicles can have protection systems that either prevent crashes from happening or reduce the severity of injuries in the event of a crash.

Vehicle safety standards are implemented at the national, regional, and global levels. The global New Car Assessment Program (NCAP) provides a safety rating for newly manufactured cars, which can be used to assess vehicle safety. It has been observed that vehicles with higher ratings are significantly safer. An issue, however, is that only a portion of vehicles globally are rated by NCAP, which may exclude older vehicles. An effective indicator should consider these issues in safety standards and safety ratings. Gitelman (2014)[29] recommends that the NCAP rating and the median age of vehicles be taken as useful indicators in assessing a country's vehicle safety. This is echoed by the GRSP, which sees the percentage of vehicles in a fleet with high quality safety standards as a useful road safety indicator (footnote 25).

In addition to this, Gitelman et al. propose an additional indicator relevant to Asia and the Pacific: the measurement of exposure, particularly to motorcycles (footnote 29). The rationale behind this is that more motorcycles might mean higher risk of severe injuries and fatalities on the road. Vehicle registration data can show the percentage of motorcycles in a fleet.

Road Infrastructure

The PIARC recommends a long list of road inventory data that can be collected for road safety (footnote 24). The list includes road class, road width and type, adjacent land use, lane number and widths, intersection of crossing type, traffic control devices, road alignment, street lighting, road surface, shoulders, speed limits, roadside hazards, and pedestrian facilities. While these are all helpful to assess road safety, establishing the link between these attributes and crash fatalities and injuries is a difficult task.

The iRAP safety star ratings provide an established methodology that assesses the safety of roads for different road users: cars, motorcycles, bicycles, and pedestrians. Each additional star in the five-star rating system denotes a safer road; a three-star road is the minimum safety rating that countries should aspire to get.

Countries can use the iRAP star rating to measure the quality of their roads, but the indicators should cover roads that have been assessed through iRAP. Recommended indicators include percentage of roads with three-star ratings or higher for a given road type and road user type. The result of this kind of exercise can be used to monitor the quality of roads and to push for the building of safer roads.

Post-Crash Response

Post-crash response refers to the medical treatment of road traffic injuries. It includes emergency response, treatment, and long-term rehabilitation. It is widely supported that post-crash response is a crucial determinant of crash fatality and severe injury risk.

The GRSP recommends the interval of response as an SPI, using as basis the percentage of crashes that receive emergency response within the country's national time interval target and those outside the time interval target (footnote 25). Such data, however, might be difficult to collect as many crashes are underreported and a lot of countries do not have coordinated emergency response systems.

---

[29] V. Gitelman et al. 2014. Development of Road Safety Indicators for the European Countries. *Advances in Social Sciences Research Journal.* 1(4), 138–158.

Because of this, the indicators recommended by Gitelman et. al. might be useful to APRSO member countries, including the number and composition of emergency medical system staff per 10,000 citizens; availability of emergency response units (e.g. ambulances); availability of trauma beds; and response time (footnote 29). These outputs are more easily measured and are useful to monitor in a country.

Table 6 summarizes the proposed SPIs to be collected at the national level, together with the recommended source of data.

Table 6   Proposed National-Level Safety Performance Indicators

Category	Safety Performance Indicators	Source of Data
Speeds	Number of speeding violations by type of road	Enforcement data
	Number of fatalities and injuries caused by speeding	Crash data
Alcohol and drugs	Number of drunk or drug driving violations	Enforcement data
	Number and percentage of severe injuries and fatalities that are caused by one road user that has a BAC exceeding the legal limit	Crash and hospital data
	Number and percentage of severe injuries and fatalities that are caused by one road user that is positive of drug use	Crash data
Safety equipment – cars	Number of sealtbelt-wearing violations	Enforcement data
	Number of child restraints violations	Enforcement data
	Number and percentage of fatalities and injuries that involve the non-use of seatbelts	Crash data
	Number and percentage of fatalities and injuries that involve the non-use of child restraints	Crash data
Safety equipment – motorcycles	Number of helmet-wearing violations	Enforcement data
	Number of fatalities and injuries that involve the non-use of helmets	Crash data
Distracted driving	Number of distracted driving violations	Enforcement data
	Number of fatalities and injuries that involve distracted driving	Crash data
Vehicles	Percentage of vehicles in a fleet with high-quality NCAP safety standards	Vehicle registration data
	Percentage of motorcycles in the vehicle fleet	Vehicle registration data
	Number of fatalities and injuries involving vehicle defects	Crash data
Road infrastructure	Percentage of roads that meet a three-star iRAP rating (or equivalent rating tool) or better for each road user type in iRAP	Lead agency for roads
Post-crash response	Number and composition of EMS staff per 10,000 citizens	Hospital data
	Availability of emergency response units (e.g. ambulances)	Hospital data
	Availability of trauma beds per 10,000 citizens	Hospital data

BAC = blood alcohol concentration, EMS = emergency medical staff, iRAP = International Road Assessment Programme, NCAP = New Car Assessment Program.
Source: Asia-Pacific Road Safety Observatory, 2021.

6. Safety Performance Indicators at the Regional Level

Choosing indicators to be collected at the regional level is more complex than selecting national-level indicators. In Asia and the Pacific, countries have varying definitions, policies, legislation, and resources when it comes to safety performance, making cross-country comparisons difficult. The most important criterion for choosing regional SPIs is the effectivity of the indicator as a comparator of performance between countries. The regional SPIs follow the same categories as the national SPIs but the indicators themselves vary.

For speed, the national indicators on speed limit compliance would not be reliable for cross-country comparison due to different speed limit laws across countries and the overall weaknesses in enforcement and crash data collection. Gitelman et. al propose the use of mean flow travel speeds, speed distribution, and speed variance for cross-country comparison (footnote 29). Free-flow average speeds and 85th-percentile speeds, disaggregated by vehicle type, road type, and time of day, could be applied. However, the challenge of comparing mean speeds by type of road is the variability of road and traffic conditions among the APRSO member countries. Because of this, the focus of speed comparisons should be on roads that are similar in the Asian context (e.g. expressways, open roads). Standard definitions and methods of collection should be established by the APRSO to guide countries in collecting these data. An initial observational study can be pursued by the APRSO in select countries as a test case.

Aside from speed limit compliance, the GRSP recommends conducting surveys to determine the percentage of vehicle drivers who admit to overspeeding in the last 30 days and the percentage of drivers who say overspeeding is acceptable (footnote 25). While useful for cross-country comparisons, these indicators can be difficult to implement as the data must be standardized, which will require a wide-scale study across APRSO countries.

For drunk and drug driving, Gitelman et. al stated that the ideal SPI for alcohol and drugs in Europe is the prevalence and concentration of different substances among the road user population (footnote 25). This indicator is ideal, but again difficult to implement in APRSO countries where there are different methods for collecting alcohol and drug-related data (e.g. some have mandatory random testing while others can only conduct testing after a series of other tests).

Given this, Gitelman et al. recommend that an initial regional SPI can be the number and percentage of severe injuries and fatalities that are caused by one road user that has a BAC exceeding the legal limit (footnote 29). In the future, this can be extended to all psychoactive substances, and testing can be made mandatory. The GRSP also recommends conducting surveys among drivers and using the percentage of drivers complying with alcohol level limits as an indicator (footnote 25). While helpful for an individual country, this will be difficult to do within the APRSO for cross-country comparison.

On safety equipment, national studies on the use of seatbelts and child restraints in vehicles and of helmets in motorcycles are proposed. Indicators should be disaggregated by time of day and type of road to allow cross-country comparison. The collection of these types of data is straightforward and often only involves roadside inspections and observations by trained observers or automatic cameras.

Similar to the data on safety equipment, data on distracted driving can be collected through a national study, and disaggregated by time of day and road user to enable comparison among countries.

Regional SPIs for vehicles and roads can be patterned after the national-level SPIs, which already follow established metrics and methodologies. Specifically, these are the NCAP rating for vehicles and the iRAP star rating for roads.

Regional indicators for post-crash response can also follow national-level indicators as these are outputs which can be used for cross-country comparison.

To summarize, Table 7 enumerates SPIs that are recommended to be collected by the APRSO from its member countries.

Table 7   **Proposed Regional-Level Safety Performance Indicators**

Category	Safety Performance Indicators	Source of Data
Speeds	Free-flow average speeds disaggregated by vehicle type, road type, and time of day.	Spot surveys
	85th-percentile speeds disaggregated by vehicle type, road type, and time of day	Spot surveys
	Percentage of vehicles exceeding the speed limit	Enforcement data and spot surveys
Alcohol	Number and percentage of severe injuries and fatalities that are caused by one road user that has a BAC exceeding the legal limit	Enforcement data
Drugs	Number and percentage of severe injuries and fatalities that are caused by one road user that is positive of drug use	Enforcement data
Helmet wearing	Percentage of motorcyclists appropriately wearing an appropriate helmet by road type	Observational studies
Seatbelt wearing	Percentage of drivers and passengers wearing a seatbelt by vehicle type and road type	Observational studies
Child restraints	Percentage of vehicles with child restraints	Observational studies
Distracted driving	Percentage of drivers using a mobile phone while driving	Observational studies/ enforcement data
Vehicles	Percentage of vehicles in a fleet with high quality NCAP safety standards	Vehicle registration
	Median age of vehicles	Vehicle registration
Roads	iRAP star rating or equivalent rating per road type and road user type	Lead agency for roads
	Percentage of roads with a three-star iRAP) rating or better	Lead agency for roads
Post-crash response	Number and composition of EMS staff per 10,000 citizens	Lead agency for health
	Availability of emergency response units per 10,000 citizens	Lead agency for health
	Availability of trauma beds per 10,000 citizens	Lead agency for health

APRSO = Asia–Pacific Road Safety Observatory, BAC = blood alcohol concentration, EMS = emergency medical staff, iRAP = International Road Assessment Programme, NCAP = New Car Assessment Program.
Source: APRSO. 2021.

7. Process and Implementation Indicators

In addition to SPIs, it is useful to compile a set of supporting information that can be used to describe the characteristics of road safety outputs in a national context, particularly on institutional management indicators.

Road safety is a public good, and as a consequence the national effort to address road safety can be identified by the financial resources allocated for road safety in a country's annual budget. Budgetary resources are likely spread across several different ministries or organizations. It is necessary to identify allocations made for (i) traffic policing; (ii) highway agency budgets for road safety elements, such as road safety audit and blackspot programs; (iii) transport agency programs for road safety; and (iv) health agency budget elements for emergency services related to road safety trauma.

Beyond the annual budget, the GRSP also identifies the following management indicators:
- Publication of a national action plan for road safety with targets.
- Establishment of a lead agency for road safety.
- Proportion of interventions that have been or are being implemented on time.
- Number of years between updates of the targets.
- Number of road safety international agreements and conventions which have been ratified or acceded to (footnote 25).

These can be collected through legal and policy instruments or other official country documents, and can apply at the national and regional levels.

Other process or implementation indicators cover outputs or legislation concerning speed, drunk driving, safety equipment, distracted driving, vehicle safety, road infrastructure, and post-crash response in line with indicators collected by WHO (footnote 9). To avoid duplication, indicators that are already provided in the WHO report can be collected in coordination with WHO. Table 8 enumerates process and implementation indicators to be collected at the national and regional level.

Table 8   **Proposed National- and Regional-Level Process and Implementation Indicators**

Category	Process or Implementation Indicator	Source
Institutional framework	Established lead agency in road safety (Yes/No)	WHO, *Global Status Report on Road Safety 2018*
	Annual budget of lead agency	Country
	Road safety unit in transport/roads/public works ministry (Yes/No)	Country
	If Yes, number of staff in road safety unit in transport/roads/public works ministry	Country
	Road safety unit in health ministry (Yes/No)	Country
	If Yes, number of staff in road safety unit in health ministry	Country
	Presence of national action plan/strategy	WHO, *Global Status Report on Road Safety 2018*
	Funding to implement strategy (full/partial/no funding)	WHO, *Global Status Report on Road Safety 2018*
	Fatality reduction target	WHO, *Global Status Report on Road Safety 2018*
	Proportion of interventions/activities implemented on time based on action plan/strategy	Country
	Number of years between updates of targets in action plan	Country
	Road safety international agreements and conventions which have been ratified or acceded to.	Country
Road infrastructure	Audits required for new road infrastructure (Yes/No)	WHO, *Global Status Report on Road Safety 2018*
	Kilometers of roads audited in a year	Country
	Presence design standards for pedestrian safety (Yes/No)	WHO, *Global Status Report on Road Safety 2018*
	Presence of design stands for cyclist safety	WHO, *Global Status Report on Road Safety 2018*
	iRAP star rating required for new road infrastructure (Yes/No)	WHO, *Global Status Report on Road Safety 2018*
	Kilometers of roads assessed through the iRAP in a year	Country
Vehicles	Total registered vehicles by vehicle type	WHO, *Global Status Report on Road Safety 2018*
	Vehicle standards (United Nations Economic Commission for Europe) applied (Yes/No)	WHO, *Global Status Report on Road Safety 2018*
Speed	Legislated speed limit per type of road	Country
Drunk driving	Legislated BAC Limit per road user (e.g. private vehicle driver, public transport driver)	Country
Drug driving	National drug-driving law (Yes/No)	WHO, *Global Status Report on Road Safety 2018*
Safety equipment – motorcycles	National motorcycle helmet law (Yes/No)	WHO, *Global Status Report on Road Safety 2018*
Safety equipment – cars	National seatbelt law (Yes/No)	WHO, *Global Status Report on Road Safety 2018*
Safety equipment – child restraints	National child restraints law (Yes/No)	WHO, *Global Status Report on Road Safety 2018*

continued on next page

Table 8   *continued*

Category	Process or Implementation Indicator	Source
Distracted driving	National distracted driving law (Yes/No)	WHO, *Global Status Report on Road Safety 2018*
Post-crash response	National emergency care access number	WHO, *Global Status Report on Road Safety 2018*
	Trauma registry	WHO, *Global Status Report on Road Safety 2018*
	Formal certification for prehospital providers	WHO, *Global Status Report on Road Safety 2018*
	National assessment of emergency care systems	WHO, *Global Status Report on Road Safety 2018*

APRSO = Asia–Pacific Road Safety Observatory, BAC = blood alcohol concentration, iRAP = International Road Assessment Programme, WHO = World Health Organization.

Source: APRSO. 2021.

8. Conclusions and Recommendations

This report enumerates indicators for the APRSO and its member countries. The indicators are aligned with key policy documents and global targets stipulated in the *12 Voluntary Global Performance Targets for Road Safety*, UN Resolution 74/299, and the Global Road Safety Facility Road Safety Management Framework. These indicators are divided into three categories: crash data elements, safety performance indicators (SPIs), and process or implementation indicators, which are further divided at the national and regional levels.

Crash data elements are proposed to be collected at the country level. These data elements have been divided into core, expanded, and integrated data so countries can gradually improve their data collection systems. At the regional level, indicators to be collected also evolve in three phases depending on the availability of the data. Initially, the APRSO will be collecting aggregate data but as data becomes available, the APRSO can collect individual and georeferenced crash records from the countries.

SPIs are also recommended for the national and regional levels. These SPIs cover speed, drunk/drug driving, safety equipment, distracted driving, road infrastructure, vehicle safety, and post-crash response. The regional SPIs differ from the national SPIs based on the effectivity of the indicator as a comparator between countries.

Finally, process or implementation indicators must cover institutional functions and legislation on key risk factors and aspects of road safety.

The Appendix contains a questionnaire that the APRSO can use to collect data from each of its member countries. This report and resources provided aim to support concrete and evidence-based interventions and solutions toward saving lives and significantly improving road safety in Asia and the Pacific.

Appendix: Sample Questionnaire for the Asia–Pacific Road Safety Observatory's Member Countries

Indicator	Data Available (Yes/No)	Response/Actual Data	Alternative Indicator with Data
Crash Data			
1. Number of fatalities and injuries per month			
2. Number of fatalities, hospitalized, and injured by road type			
3. Number of fatalities, hospitalized, and injured by vehicle type and age of person involved			
4. Number of fatalities, hospitalized, and injured by vehicle type			
5. Number of females/males killed at each age in yearly interval			
6. Number of drivers/passengers/unknown seating position of passenger cars/goods/light goods/articulated and non-articulated heavy goods killed			
Safety Performance Indicators			
7. Free-flow average speeds and disaggregated by vehicle type, road type, and time of day.			
8. 85th-percentile speeds disaggregated by vehicle type, road type, and time of day			
9. Percentage of vehicles exceeding the speed limit			
10. Number and percentage of severe injuries and fatalities that are caused by one road user that has a blood alcohol concentration (BAC) exceeding the legal limit			
11. Number and percentage of severe injuries and fatalities that are caused by one road user that is positive for drug use			
12. Percentage of motorcyclists wearing an appropriate helmet by road type			
13. Percentage of drivers and passengers wearing a seatbelt by vehicle type and road type			
14. Percentage of vehicles with appropriate child restraints			
15. Percentage of drivers using a mobile phone while driving			
16. Percentage of vehicles in a fleet with high-quality New Car Assessment Program (NCAP) safety standards			
17. Median age of vehicles			
18. International Road Assessment Programme (iRAP) star rating per road type and road user type			
19. Percentage of roads that meet a three-star iRAP rating or better			
20. Number and composition of emergency medical staff (EMS) staff per 10,000 citizens			
21. Availability of emergency response units per 10,000 citizens			
22. Availability of trauma beds per 10,000 citizens			

continued on next page

Appendix   *continued*

Indicator	Data Available (Yes/No)	Response/Actual Data	Alternative Indicator with Data
Process or Implementation Indicators			
23. Annual budget of lead agency in road safety			
24. Road safety unit in transport/roads/public works ministry (Yes/No)			
25. If "Yes," number of staff in road safety unit in Transport/ Roads/Public Works Ministry			
26. Road safety unit in health ministry (Yes/No)			
27. If "Yes," number of staff in road safety unit in health ministry			
28. Proportion of interventions/activities implemented or are being implemented on time based on action plan/strategy			
29. Number of years between updates of targets in action plan			
30. Road safety international agreements and conventions which have been ratified or acceded to.			
31. Kilometers of roads audited in a year			
32. Kilometers of roads assessed in iRAP in a year			
33. Kilometers of roads upgraded with safety interventions in a year			
34. Legislated speed limit per type of road			
35. Legislated BAC Limit per road user (e.g. private vehicle driver, public transport driver)			

References

Asia–Pacific Road Safety Observatory (APRSO). APRSO Task Force Report on Crash Data Systems. Unpublished.

APRSO. *Minimum Set of Indicators*. https://www.unescap.org/sites/default/files/Crash-related%20minimum%20 data%20set%20and%20data%20sources.pdf.

Bliss, T. and J. Breen. 2013. *Implementing the Recommendations of the World Report: Road Safety Management Capacity Reviews and Safe System Projects Guidelines (English)*. Washington DC: World Bank Group.

Congelton, R. and W. Sweetser. 1992. Political Deadlocks and Distributional Information: The Value of the Veil. *Public Choice*, 73, 1–19.

Duc, N., D. Hoa, N. Huong, and N. Bao. 2011. Study on Quality of Existing Traffic Accident Data in Vietnam. *Proceedings of the Eastern Asia Society for Transportation Studies*. https://www.academia. edu/4140898/Study_on_Quality_of_Existing_Traffic_Accident_Data_in_Vietnam.

European Commission. 2018. *Common Accident Data Set*. https://ec.europa.eu/transport/road_safety/system/ files/2021-07/cadas_glossary_v_3_7.pdf.

European Road Safety Observatory. 2021. *Annual statistical report on road safety in the EU 2020*. https://ec.europa. eu/transport/road_safety/statistics-and-analysis/data-and-analysis/annual-statistical-report_en.

Gitelman, V., M. Vis, W. Weijermars, and S. Hakker. 2014. Development of Road Safety Indicators for the European Countries. *Advances in Social Sciences Research Journal*. 1(4), 138–158.

Global Road Safety Partnership. 2020. *Towards the 12 Global Road Safety Performance Targets*. https://www. grsproadsafety.org/wp-content/uploads/Towards-the-12-Voluntary-Global-Targets-for-Road-Safety.pdf.

Government of the United Kingdom, Department of Environment, Transport and the Regions. 2000. *New Directions in Speed Management – A Review of Policy*. London: Department of Environment, Transport and the Regions.

Gudmundsson, H., R. Hall, G. Marsden, and J. Zeitsman. 2016. *Sustainable Transportation: Indicators, Frameworks, and Performance Management*. Berlin Heidelberg: Springer-Verlag.

Gühnemann, A. 2016. *SUMP Manual on Monitoring and Evaluation: Assessing the Impact of Measures and Evaluating Mobility Planning Processes*. www.sump-challenges.eu/kits.

Hills, D. and K. Junge. 2010. *Guidance for Transport Impact Evaluations: Choosing an Evaluation Approach to Achieve Better Attribution*. UK: Tavistock Institute.

International Transport Forum. 2019. *Road Safety Annual Report 2019*. https://www.itf-oecd.org/sites/default/files/docs/irtad-road-safety-annual-report-2019.pdf.

Johns Hopkins School of Public Health. 2020. *Presentation on Risk Factors*.

Montella, A., D. Andreassen, A. Tarko, S. Turner, F. Mauriello, L. Imbriani, M. Romero, and R. Singh. 2012. Critical Review of the International Crash Databases and Proposals for Improvement of the Italian National Database. *Procedia - Social and Behavioral Sciences*, 53, pp.49–61. https://www.sciencedirect.com/science/article/pii/S1877042812043212.

Rolison, J. 2020. Identifying the causes of road traffic collisions: Using police officers' expertise to improve the reporting of contributory factors data. *Accident Analysis and Prevention*. https://www.sciencedirect.com/science/article/pii/S0001457519311650.

State of New Jersey Police Crash Investigation Report. https://www.state.nj.us/transportation/refdata/accident/pdf/NJTR-1.pdf.

Thomas, P., R. Welsh, K. Folla, A. Laiou, S. Mavromatis, G. Yannis, D. Usami, and E. Meta. 2018. *Recommendations for a Common Data Collection System and Definitions*. SaferAfrica Project. https://www.ssatp.org/sites/ssatp/files/publication/common_data_collection_system_definitions.pdf.

Toroyan, T. and M. Peden, eds. 2007. *Youth and Road Safety*. Geneva: World Health Organization.

Turner, B., M. Tziotis, P. Hillier, D. Beck, and T. Makwasha. 2015. *Guide to Road Safety Part 8: Treatment of Crash Locations*. Australia: Austroads.

United Nations General Assembly. 2020. *UN Resolution 74/299*. https://undocs.org/en/A/RES/74/299.

United States Department of Transportation and National Highway Traffic Safety Administration. 2017. *Model Minimum Uniform Crash Criteria Fifth Edition (2017)*. https://www.nhtsa.gov/mmucc-1.

Valdez, A. 2020. *Evaluation of Electronic Road Incident Record Application and Trial in the Philippines*. Manila: Intelligent Transport System Laboratory, University of the Philippines Diliman.

Villegas, M. 2011. *CARE Databse*. https://www.unece.org/fileadmin/DAM/trans/doc/2011/wp6/ECE-TRANS-WP6-2011-pres08e.pdf.

World Health Organization (WHO). 2018. *Global Status Report on Road Safety 2018*. Geneva: World Health Organization.

WHO. 2017. *Global Road Safety Performance Targets*. https://www.who.int/violence_injury_prevention/road_traffic/12GlobalRoadSafetyTargets.pdf.

WHO. 2010. *Data Systems: A Road Safety Manual for Decision-Makers and Practitioners*. https://www.who.int/roadsafety/projects/manuals/data/en/.

World Road Association. 2019. *Road Safety Manual - World Road Association (PIARC)*. https://roadsafety.piarc.org/en.

www.ingramcontent.com/pod-product-compliance
Lightning Source LLC
Chambersburg PA
CBHW042035220326
41599CB00045BA/7405